# WITH
# EACH
# &
# EVERY
# BREATH

A GUIDE TO MEDITATION

*Thanissaro Bhikkhu*
*(Geoffrey DeGraff)*

*for free distribution*

INQUIRIES MAY BE ADDRESSED TO:

The Abbot
Metta Forest Monastery
PO Box 1409
Valley Center, CA 92082
USA

# Contents

# Introduction

## MEDITATION: WHAT & WHY

Meditation is training for the mind, to help it develop the strengths and skills it needs to solve its problems. Just as there are many different remedies for the various illnesses of the body, there are many different types of meditation for the various problems of the mind.

The meditation technique taught in this book is a skill aimed at solving the mind's most basic problem: the stress and suffering it brings on itself through its own thoughts and actions. Even though the mind wants happiness, it still manages to weigh itself down with mental pain. In fact, that pain comes from the mind's misguided efforts to find happiness. Meditation helps to uncover the reasons for why the mind does this and, in uncovering them, helps you to cure them. In curing them, it opens you to the possibility of genuine happiness, a happiness you can rely on, a happiness that will never change or let you down.

That's the good news of meditation: Genuine happiness is possible, and you can reach it through your own efforts. You don't have to content yourself only with pleasures that will eventually leave you. You don't have to resign yourself to the idea that temporary happiness is the best life has to offer. And you don't have to pin your hopes for happiness on any person or power outside yourself. You can train the mind to access a totally reliable happiness, a happiness that causes no harm to you or to anyone else.

Not only is the *goal* of meditation good; the *means* for attaining that goal are good as well. They're activities and mental qualities you can be proud to develop: things like honesty, integrity, compassion, mindfulness, and discernment. Because true happiness comes from within, it doesn't require that you take anything from anyone else. Your true happiness doesn't conflict with the true happiness of anyone else in the world. And when you find true happiness inside, you have more to share with others.

This is why the practice of meditation is an act of kindness for others as well as for yourself. When you solve the problem of stress and suffering, you, of course, are the person who will most directly benefit. But you aren't the only one. This is because when you create stress and suffering for yourself, you weaken yourself. You place burdens not only on yourself but also on the people around you: both by having to depend on them for help and support, and also by damaging them with the foolish things you might do or say out of weakness and fear. At the same time, you're hampered from helping them with their problems, for your hands are filled with your own. But if your mind can learn how to stop causing itself stress and suffering, you're less of a burden on others and you're in a better position to give them a helping hand.

So the practice of meditation teaches you to respect the things within you that are worthy of respect: your desire for a genuine happiness, totally reliable and totally harmless; and your ability to find that happiness through your own efforts.

To bring a total end to the mind's self-inflicted stress and suffering requires a great deal of dedication, training, and skill. But the meditation technique taught in this book doesn't give its benefits only to people who are ready to follow it all the way to the total cure of awakening. Even if you simply want help in managing pain or finding a little more peace and stability in your life, meditation has plenty to offer you. It can also strengthen the mind to deal with many of the problems of day-to-day life, because it develops qualities like mindfulness, alertness, concentration, and discernment that are useful in all activities, at home, at work, or wherever you are. These qualities are also helpful in dealing with some of the larger, more difficult issues of life.

Addiction, trauma, loss, disappointment, illness, aging, and even death are a lot easier to handle when the mind has developed the skills fostered by meditation. So even if you don't make it all the way to total freedom from stress and suffering, meditation can help you to handle your sufferings more skillfully—in other words, with less harm to yourself and the people around you. This, in itself, is a worthwhile use of your time. If you then decide to pursue the meditation further, to see if it really can lead to total freedom, so much the better.

## WHAT'S IN THIS BOOK

The meditation technique described here is drawn from two sources. The first source is the Buddha's set of instructions on how to use the breath in training the mind. These instructions are found in the Pali Canon, the oldest extant record of the Buddha's teachings. As the Canon states, the Buddha found the breath to be a restful meditation topic—both for body and mind—as well as an ideal topic for developing mindfulness, concentration, and discernment. In fact, it was the topic he himself used on the path to his awakening. That's why he recommended it to more people and taught it in more detail than any other topic of meditation.

The second source is a method of breath meditation developed in the last century by Ajaan Lee Dhammadharo, a master of a branch of Buddhism known in Thailand as the Wilderness Tradition. Ajaan Lee's method builds on the Buddha's instructions, explaining in detail many of the points that the Buddha left in a condensed form. I trained in this technique for ten years under Ajaan Fuang Jotiko, one of Ajaan Lee's students, so some of the insights here come from my training with Ajaan Fuang as well.

I've followed these sources in focusing on the breath as the main topic of meditation because it's the safest of all meditation topics. The technique described here brings the body and mind to a balanced state of well-being. This in turn allows the mind to gain balanced insights into its own workings, so that it can see the ways in which it's causing stress and suffering, and let them go effectively.

This technique is part of a comprehensive path of mind training that involves not only meditation but also the development of generosity and virtue. The basic approach in each part of this training is the same: to understand all your actions as part of a chain of causes and effects, so that you can direct the causes in a more positive direction. With every action in thought, word, or deed, you reflect on what you're doing while you're doing it. You look for the motivation leading to your actions, and the results your actions give rise to. As you reflect, you learn to question your actions in a specific way:

- Do they lead to stress and suffering, or to the end of stress and suffering?
- If they lead to stress, are they necessary?
- If not, why do them again?
- If they lead to the end of stress, how can you master them as skills?

Training in virtue and generosity asks these questions of your words and deeds. Training in meditation approaches all events in the mind as actions—whether they're thoughts or emotions—and questions them in the same way. In other words, it forces you to look at your thoughts and emotions less in terms of their content, and more in terms of where they come from and where they lead.

This strategy of observing your actions and probing them with these questions is directly related to the problem it's meant to solve: the stresses and sufferings caused by your actions. That's why it underlies the training as a whole. Meditation simply allows you to observe your actions more carefully, and to uncover and abandon ever more subtle levels of stress caused by those actions.

It also develops the mental qualities that strengthen your ability to act in skillful ways.

Although the meditation technique described here is part of a specifically Buddhist training, you don't have to be Buddhist to follow it. It can help in overcoming problems that aren't specific to Buddhists. After all, Buddhists aren't the only people who cause themselves stress and suffering, and the qualities of mind developed through meditation don't have a Buddhist copyright. Mindfulness, alertness, concentration, and discernment benefit everyone who develops them. All that's asked is that you give these qualities a serious try.

The purpose of this book is to present the practice of meditation—along with the larger training of which it's a part—in a way that's easy to read and to put into practice. The book is divided into five parts, each part followed by a list of additional resources available at **accesstoinsight.org** and **dhammatalks.org** that will help you explore the issues discussed in that part in more detail.

The first part of the book contains instructions in the basic steps of how to meditate. The second part gives advice on how to deal with some of the problems that may come up as you practice. The third part deals with issues that arise as you try to make meditation a part of your life as a whole. The fourth part deals with issues that arise as your meditation progresses to a higher level of skill. The fifth part deals with how to choose and relate to a meditation teacher who can give you the type of personalized training no book can possibly provide.

## HOW TO READ THIS BOOK

I've tried to cover most of the issues that a committed meditator will encounter in a self-directed practice. For this reason, *if you're brand new to meditation* and are not yet ready to commit to a serious practice, you will find more material in this book than you'll immediately need. Still, you can find plenty of useful guidance here if you *read selectively.* A good approach would be to read just what's necessary to get started meditating and then put the book down to give it a try.

*To get started:*

1) Read the discussion of "Breath" in the following section (pages 17 to 19), down to the heading, "Why the breath."

2) Skip to the section titled, "Focusing on the Breath" in Part One (pages 39 to 46). Read the six steps listed there until you can hold them in mind. Then find a comfortable place to sit and try following as many of the steps as you feel comfortable attempting. If the steps are too detailed for you, read the article, "A Guided Meditation," listed at the end of Part One, or sit down and meditate while listening to any of the audio files with the same title available on www.dhammatalks.org.

3) If you encounter problems as you get started, return to Part One and also consult Part Two.

As for the rest of the book, you can save that till later, when you're ready to raise the level of your commitment.

Even then, it will be wise to read the book selectively—especially Part Three. There the advice is again aimed at a fully committed meditator. Some of it may involve more commitment than you're ready to make, so take whatever advice seems practical in the context of your current life and values, and leave the rest for other people—or for yourself at a later time.

Remember, *nothing in the practice of meditation is ever forced on you.* The only compulsion comes from an inner force: your own desire to be free from self-inflicted suffering and stress.

## BASIC PREMISES

When you want to master a meditation technique, it's good to know the premises underlying the technique. That way you have a clear idea of what you're getting into. Knowing the premises also helps you understand how and why the technique is supposed to work. If you have doubts about the premises, you can try them on as working hypotheses, to see if they really do help in dealing with the problems of stress and suffering. Meditation doesn't require that you swear allegiance to anything you can't fully understand. But it does ask you to give its premises a serious try.

As your meditation progresses, you can apply the basic premises to areas that come up in your meditation that aren't explained in the book. In this way, the meditation becomes less of a foreign technique, and more of your own path in exploring the mind and solving its problems as they arise.

Because breath meditation is a training in which the mind focuses on the breath, its basic premises focus on two topics: the workings of the mind, and the workings of the breath.

*Mind.* The word "mind" here covers not only the intellectual side of the mind, but also its emotional side together with its will to act. In other words, the word "mind" covers what we normally think of as "heart" as well.

The mind is not passive. Because it's responsible for a body with many needs, it has to take an active approach to experience. Its actions shape its experience as it looks for food, both mental and physical, to keep itself and the body nourished. It's driven by hungers both physical and mental. We're all familiar with the need to feed physically. Mentally, the mind feeds both externally and internally on relationships and emotions. Externally, it hungers for such things as love, recognition, status, power, wealth, and praise. Internally, it feeds off its love for others and its own self-esteem, as well as the pleasures that come from emotions both healthy and not: honor, gratitude, greed, lust, and anger.

At any given moment, the mind is presented with a wide range of sights, sounds, smells, tastes, tactile sensations, and ideas. From this range, it chooses which things to focus attention on and which to ignore in its search for food. These choices shape the world of its experience. This is why, if you and I walk through a store at the same time, for example, we will experience different stores to the extent that we're looking for different things.

The mind's search for nourishment is constant and never-ending, because its food—especially its mental food—is always threatening to run out. Whatever satisfaction it derives from its food is always short-lived. No sooner has the mind found a place to feed than it's already looking for where to feed next. Should it stay here? Should it go somewhere else? These incessant questions of "What next?" "Where next?" drive its search for well-being. But because these questions are the *questions of hunger,* they themselves keep eating away at the mind. Driven by hunger to keep answering these questions, the mind often acts compulsively— sometimes willfully—out of ignorance, misunderstanding what causes unnecessary stress and what doesn't. This causes it to create even more suffering and stress.

The purpose of meditation is to end this ignorance, and to root out the questions of hunger that keep driving it.

An important aspect of this ignorance is the mind's blindness to its own inner workings in the present moment, for the present moment is where choices are made. Although the mind often acts under the force of habit, it doesn't have to. It has the option of making new choices with every moment. The more clearly you see what's happening in the present, the more likely you are to make skillful choices: ones that will lead to genuine happiness— and, with practice, will bring you closer and closer to total freedom from suffering and stress—now and into the future. Meditation focuses your attention on the present moment because the present moment is where you can watch the workings of the mind and direct them in a more skillful direction. The present is the only moment in time where you can act and bring about change.

**The committee of the mind.** One of the first things you learn about the mind as you get started in meditation is that *it has many minds*. This is because you have many different ideas about how to satisfy your hungers and find well-being, and many different desires based on those ideas. These ideas boil down to different notions about what constitutes happiness, where it can be found, and what you are as a person: your needs for particular kinds of pleasure, and your abilities to provide those pleasures. Each desire thus acts as a seed for a particular sense of who you are and the world you live in.

The Buddha had a technical term for this sense of self-identity in a particular world of experience: He called it *becoming*. Take note of this term and the concept behind it, for it's central to understanding why you cause yourself stress and suffering and what's involved in learning how to stop.

If the concept seems foreign to you, think of when you're drifting off to sleep and an image of a place appears in the mind. You enter into the image, lose touch with the world outside, and that's when you've entered the world of a dream. That world of a dream, plus your sense of having entered into it, is a form of becoming.

Once you become sensitive to this process, you'll see that you engage in it even when you're awake, and many times in the course of a day. To gain freedom from the stress and suffering it can cause, you're going to have to examine the many becomings you create in your search for food—the selves spawned by your desires, and the worlds they inhabit—for only when you've examined these things thoroughly can you gain release from their limitations.

You'll find that, in some cases, different desires share common ideas of what happiness is and who you are (such as your desires for establishing a safe and stable family). In others, their ideas conflict (as when your desires for your family conflict with your desires for immediate pleasure regardless of the consequences). Some of your desires relate to the same mental worlds; others to conflicting mental worlds; and still others to mental worlds totally divorced from one another. The same goes for the different senses of "you" inhabiting each of those worlds. Some of your "yous" are in harmony, others are incompatible, and still others are totally unrelated to one another.

So there are many different ideas of "you" in your mind, each with its own agenda. Each of these "yous" is a member of the committee of the mind. This is why the mind is less like a single mind and more like an unruly throng of people: lots of different voices, with lots of different opinions about what you should do.

Some members of the committee are open and honest about the assumptions underlying their central desires. Others are more obscure and devious. This is because each committee member is like a politician, with its own supporters and strategies for satisfying their desires. Some committee members are idealistic and honorable. Others are not. So the mind's committee is less like a communion of saints planning a charity event, and more like a corrupt city council, with the balance of power constantly shifting between different factions, and many deals being made in back rooms.

One of the purposes of meditation is to bring these dealings out into the open, so that you can bring more order to the committee—so that your desires for happiness work less at cross purposes, and more in harmony as you realize that they don't always have to be in conflict. Thinking of these desires as a committee also helps you realize that when the practice of meditation goes against some of your desires, it doesn't go against *all* of your desires. You're not being starved. You don't have to identify with the desires being thwarted through meditation, because you have other, more skillful desires to identify with. The choice is yours. You can also use the more skillful members of the committee to train the less skillful ones so that they stop sabotaging your efforts to find a genuine happiness.

*Always remember that genuine happiness is possible, and the mind can train itself to find that happiness.* These are probably the most important premises underlying the practice of breath meditation. There are many dimensions to the mind, dimensions often obscured by the squabbling of the committee members and their fixation with fleeting forms of happiness. One of those dimensions is totally *unconditioned.* In other words, it's not dependent on conditions at all. It's not affected by space or time. It's an experience of total, unalloyed freedom and happiness. This is because it's free from hunger and from the need to feed.

But even though this dimension is unconditioned, it can be attained by changing the *conditions* in the mind: developing the skillful members of the committee so that your choices become more and more conducive to genuine happiness.

This is why the path of meditation is called a path: It's like the path to a mountain. Even though the path doesn't cause the mountain, and your walking on the path doesn't cause the mountain, the act of walking along the path can take you to the mountain.

Or you can think of the unconditioned dimension as like the fresh water in salt water. The ordinary mind is like salt water, which makes you sick when you drink it. If you simply let the salt water sit still, the fresh water won't separate out on its own. You have to make an effort to distill it. The act of distilling doesn't create fresh water. It simply brings out the fresh water already there, providing you with all the nourishment you need to quench your thirst.

**Training the mind.** The training that gets you to the mountain and provides you with fresh water has three aspects: virtue, concentration, and discernment. Virtue is the skill with which you interact with other people and living beings at large, based on the intention to cause no harm to yourself or to others. This is a topic that we will consider in Part Three, in the discussion of issues that commonly arise when integrating meditation into daily life, but it's important to note here why virtue is related to meditation. If you act in harmful ways, then when you sit down to meditate, the knowledge of that harm gets in the way of staying firmly in the present moment. If you react with regret over the harm you've done, you find it difficult to stay settled in the present moment with confidence. If you react with denial, you build inner walls in your awareness that create more opportunities for ignorance and make it harder to look directly at what's really going on in the mind.

The best way to avoid these two reactions is to stick to the intention not to do anything harmful in the first place, and then make up your mind to follow that intention with more and more skill. If you've seen that you have acted unskillfully, acknowledge your mistake, recognize that regret won't erase the mistake, and resolve not to repeat that mistake in the future. This is the most that can be asked of a human being living in time, where our actions aimed at shaping the future can be based only on knowledge of the past and present.

The second aspect of the training is concentration. Concentration is the skill of keeping the mind centered on a single object, such as the breath, with a sense of ease, refreshment, and equanimity—equanimity being the ability to watch things without falling under the sway of likes and dislikes.

Attaining concentration requires developing three qualities of mind:

• *Alertness*—the ability to know what's happening in the body and mind while it's happening.

• *Ardency*—the desire and effort to abandon any unskillful qualities that may arise in the mind, and to develop skillful qualities in their place.

• *Mindfulness*—the ability to keep something in mind. In the case of breath meditation, this means remembering to stay with the breath and to maintain the qualities of alertness and ardency with every in-and-out breath.

When these three qualities become strong, they can bring the mind to a state of strong concentration called *jhana,* or meditative absorption, which we will discuss in Part Four. Because jhana is based on desire—the desire to develop skillful qualities in the mind—it, too, is a form of becoming. But it's a special form of becoming that allows you to see the *processes* of becoming in action. At the same time, the ease and refreshment provided by jhana are health food for the mind, enabling you to abandon many of the unskillful eating habits that would pull you off the path. Because the supply of mental food coming from jhana is steady, it takes some of the pressure off of your need to feed. This allows you to step back from the questions of hunger, and to look at them through the *questions of discernment:* seeing where the stress of feeding is unnecessary, and how you can master the skills to go beyond it. This is why jhana is central to the path of training.

The third aspect of the training is discernment. Discernment is the ability:

• to distinguish the skillful processes in the mind from the unskillful ones,

• to understand how to abandon what's unskillful and to develop what's skillful, and

• to know how to motivate yourself so that you can abandon unskillful processes and to develop skillful processes even when you're not in the mood.

You learn these three abilities by listening to others—as when you read a book like this one—and by observing your own actions and asking the right questions about them. In the beginning, you step back from the questions of hunger—which demand an answer *right now* as to where and what to feed on next—and take stock of how you've been feeding:

> In what ways do your feeding habits lead to stress?
> In what ways is that stress unnecessary?
> To what extent is it worth it—in other words, to what extent does the pleasure gained from feeding compensate for the stress?

In the beginning stages, as you develop virtue and try to master concentration, the questions of discernment are simply looking for better ways to feed. In other words, they're refined versions of the questions of hunger. You come to realize that the pleasure you gained from carelessly acting in harmful ways or letting the mind wander where it will isn't worth the stress it entails. You begin to see where the stress you thought was unavoidable isn't really necessary. You have other, better ways of finding inner nourishment, feeding on the higher pleasures that virtue and concentration provide.

As your concentration develops, your discernment into the levels of stress in the mind gets more and more refined, so that your sense of what is and isn't skillful gets more refined as well. As you keep applying the questions of discernment even to your practice of jhana, you begin to wonder if it might be possible to escape the stress that comes even with the most refined sort of feeding. What sort of skill would that involve?

This is where the questions of discernment are no longer just a refined version of the questions of hunger. They become *noble* questions in that they take you beyond the need to feed. They bring dignity to your search for happiness. They help you uncover the dimension where even feeding on jhana is no longer necessary. And when that dimension is finally uncovered, all stress comes to an end.

The questions of noble discernment—concerning unnecessary stress, the actions that cause it, and the actions that can help put an end to it—are related to one of the Buddha's most famous teachings: *the four noble truths*. The fact of unnecessary stress is the first truth; the unskillful mental actions that cause it are the second; the fact that it can come to an end is the third; and the skillful actions that bring it to an end are the fourth. These truths are noble for three reasons. One, they're absolute. They're true for everyone everywhere, so they're not just a matter of personal opinion or your cultural background.

Two, they provide guidance for a noble path of practice. They teach you not to deny or run away from the stress you're causing, but to acknowledge it and face it until you comprehend it. When you comprehend it, you can see the causes of that stress in your actions and abandon them. You develop the skillful actions that put an end to stress so that you can realize freedom from stress for yourself.

The third reason these truths are noble is that, when you use the questions underlying them to examine and question your actions, they lead ultimately to a noble attainment: a genuine happiness that puts an end to the need to feed, and so causes no harm to anyone at all.

Because discernment is aimed at bringing your actions to the highest level of skill, it grows directly out of the quality of *ardency* in your concentration. However, it also builds on *alertness* in seeing which actions lead to which results. And it informs *mindfulness,* so that you can remember the lessons you've learned from what you've observed and can apply them in the future.

In fact, all three aspects of the training—virtue, concentration, and discernment—help one another along. Virtue makes it easier to settle down in concentration and to be honest with yourself in discerning which members of the mind's committee are skillful and which ones are not. Concentration provides the mind with a sense of refreshment that allows it to resist unskillful urges that would create lapses in virtue, and the stability it needs to discern clearly what's actually going on inside. Discernment provides strategies for developing virtue, along with an understanding of the mind's workings that allow it to settle down in ever-stronger states of concentration.

Virtue, concentration, and discernment, in turn, are all based on the most fundamental part of the training: the practice of generosity. In being generous with your belongings, your time, your energy, your knowledge, and your forgiveness, you create a space of freedom in the mind. Instead of being driven by your various appetites, you can step back and realize the joy that comes when you're not a slave to hunger all the time. This realization provides your basic impetus to look for a happiness where you don't need to feed at all. Seeing the good that comes from giving, you can learn to approach the practice of virtue and meditation not just with an eye to what you can get out of it, but also with an eye to what you can *give* to the practice. The training of the mind becomes a gift both for yourself and for the people around you.

So, all in all, the premises of breath meditation are based on four observations about the mind that the Buddha called *noble truths:*

1) The mind experiences stress and suffering.

2) The stress and suffering come from the way the mind shapes its experience through its actions driven by ignorance.

3) That ignorance can be ended, opening your awareness to an unconditioned dimension free of stress and suffering.

4) That dimension, even though it's unconditioned, can be reached by training the mind in the skillful qualities of virtue, concentration, and discernment.

The purpose of breath meditation is to help with that training.

*Breath.* The word "breath" covers a wide range of energies in the body. Most prominently, there's the energy of the in-and-out breath. We tend to think of this breath as the air coming in and out of the lungs, but this air wouldn't move if it weren't for an energy in the body activating the muscles that draw it in and allow it to go out. When you meditate on the in-and-out breath, you may start by paying attention to the movement of the air, but as your sensitivity develops, you become more focused on the energy.

In addition to the energy of the in-and-out breath, there are subtler flows of energy that spread through all parts of the body. These can be experienced as the mind grows more still. There are two types: moving energies; and still, steady energies. The moving energies are directly related to the energy of the in-and-out breath. For instance, there is the flow of energy in the nerves, as all the muscles involved in breathing, however subtly, are activated with each breath. This energy flow also allows you to have sensation in the different parts of the body and to move them at will. There is also the flow of energy that nourishes the heart with each breath, and then spreads from the heart as it pumps the blood. This can be felt with the movement of blood through the blood vessels and out to every pore of the skin.

As for the still, steady energies, these are centered in different spots in the body, such as the tip of the breastbone, the middle of the brain, the palms of the hands, or the soles of the feet. Once the in-and-out breath grows calm, these energies can be spread to fill the whole body with a sense of stillness and fullness that feels solid and secure.

To some people, these energies in the different parts of the body might seem mysterious—or even imaginary. But even if the concept of these energies seems foreign to you, the energies themselves are not. They form the way you directly experience the body from within. If they weren't already there, you wouldn't have any sense of where your own body is.

So when you try to acquaint yourself with these energies, there are three points to keep in mind:

*1) You're not concerned with your breath as it might be observed by a doctor or a machine outside you.* You're concerned with your breath as only you can know it: as part of your direct experience of having a body. If you have trouble thinking of these energies as "breath," see if thinking of them as "breathing sensations" or "body sensations" helps—whatever enables you to get in touch with what's actually there.

*2) This is NOT a matter of trying to create sensations that don't already exist.* You're simply making yourself more sensitive to sensations that are already there. When you're told to let the breath energies flow into one another, ask yourself if the sensations you feel seem unconnected to one another. If they do, simply hold in mind the possibility that they can connect on their own. This is what it means to *allow* them to flow.

*3) These energies are not air.* They're energy. If, while you're allowing the breath energies to spread through the various parts of the body, you sense that you're trying to force energy into those parts, stop and remind yourself: Energy doesn't need to be forced. There's plenty of space even in the most solid parts of the body for this energy to flow, so you don't have to push it against any resistance. If there's a sense of resistance to the energy, it's coming from the way you visualize it. Try to visualize the energy in a way that can slip around and through everything with ease.

The best way to get in touch with these energies is to close your eyes, notice the sensations that tell you where the different parts of your body are, and then allow yourself to view those sensations as a type of energy. As you get more sensitive to those sensations and see how they interact with the energy of the in-and-out breath, it will seem more and more natural to regard them as types of breath energy. That allows you to get the most use out of them.

**Why the breath.** There are two reasons why the breath is chosen as a topic of meditation: It's a good theme for developing the qualities needed for *(1) concentration* and *(2) discernment.*

1) All three qualities needed for concentration are easily developed by focusing on the breath:

*Alertness:* The only breath you can observe is the breath in the present. When you're with the breath, your attention has to be in the present. Only in the present can you observe what's going on in the body and mind as it's actually happening.

The breath is also a meditation theme that goes along with you wherever you go. As long as you're alive, you've got the breath right here to focus on. This means that you can meditate on the breath and develop alertness at any time and in any situation.

*Mindfulness:* Because the breath is so close to your present awareness, it's easy to remember. If you forget to stay with the breath, the simple sensation of an in-breath can remind you to come back to it.

*Ardency:* The breath is one of the few processes in the body over which you can exert conscious control. An important part of breath meditation is learning how to make skillful use of this fact. You can learn which ways of breathing foster pleasant sensations in the body, and which ones foster unpleasant ones. You learn a sense of time and place: when and how to change the breath to make it more comfortable, and when to leave it alone. As you develop this knowledge, you can use it as an aid in developing skillful qualities of mind.

This sort of knowledge comes from experimenting with the breath and learning to observe the effects of different kinds of breathing on the body and mind. You can call this sort of experimentation *working* with the breath, for you've got an ardent purpose: the training of the mind. But you can also call it *playing* with the breath, for it requires that you use your imagination and ingenuity in thinking of different ways to breathe and to picture the breath energy to yourself. At the same time, it can be a lot of fun as you learn to explore and discover things about your body on your own.

There are many ways in which working and playing with the breath can help foster the quality of ardency in your meditation. For instance, when you learn how to breathe in ways that feel comfortable—to energize the body when you feel tired, or to relax the body when you feel tense—you make it easier to settle into the present moment and to stay there with a sense of well-being. You learn to view the meditation not as a chore, but as an opportunity to develop an immediate sense of well-being. This gives energy to your desire to stick with the meditation over the long term.

Playing with the breath also helps you stay in the present—and stick with the meditation over time—because it gives you something interesting and engaging to do that can show immediate benefits. This keeps you from getting bored with the meditation. As you see the good results arising from adjusting the breath, you become more motivated to explore the potentials of the breath in a wide variety of different situations: how to adjust the breath when you're sick, how to adjust it when you feel physically or emotionally threatened, how to adjust it when you need to tap into reserves of energy to overcome feelings of exhaustion.

The pleasure and refreshment that can come from working and playing with the breath provide your ardency with a source of inner food. This inner food helps you deal with the obstreperous members of the committee of the mind who won't back down unless they get immediate gratification. You learn that simply breathing in a particular way gives rise to an immediate sense of pleasure. You can relax patterns of tension in different parts of the body—the back of the hands, the feet, in your stomach or chest—

that would otherwise trigger and feed unskillful urges. This alleviates the sense of inner hunger that can drive you to do things that you know aren't skillful. So in addition to helping with your ardency, this way of working with the breath can help with your practice of virtue.

2) Because of the direct connection between ardency and discernment, the act of working and playing with the breath also helps develop discernment.

• *The breath is the perfect place from which to watch the mind, for it's the physical process most responsive to the mind's own workings.* As you grow more sensitive to the breath, you'll come to see that subtle changes in the breath are often a sign of subtle changes in the mind. This can alert you to developments in the mind just as they're starting to happen. And that can help you to see more quickly through the ignorance that can lead to stress and suffering.

• *The sense of well-being fostered by working and playing with the breath gives you a solid foundation for observing stress and suffering.* If you feel threatened by your suffering, you won't have the patience and endurance needed to watch and comprehend it. As soon as you encounter it, you want to run away. But if you're dwelling in a sense of well-being in the body and mind, you don't feel so threatened by pain or suffering. That enables you to watch pain and suffering more steadily. You know that you have a safe place in your body where the breath feels comfortable, where you can focus your attention when the stress or suffering becomes too overwhelming. (For more on this topic, see the discussion of "Pain" in Part Three.) This gives you confidence to probe more deeply into the pain.

• *The sense of pleasure that comes from concentration, as it gets more refined, allows you to see more subtle levels of stress in the mind.* It's like making yourself very quiet so that you can hear subtle sounds very far away.

• *Being able to attain this inner level of pleasure puts the mind in a much better mood,* so that it's much more willing to accept the fact that it has been causing itself suffering. Training the mind to look honestly at its unskillful qualities is like talking to a person about his faults and shortcomings. If he's hungry, tired, and grumpy, he won't want to hear anything of what you have to say. You need to wait until he's well-fed and well-rested. That's when he'll be more willing to admit his faults.

This is the main issue with the mind: It's causing itself suffering through its own stupidity, its own lack of skill, and usually it doesn't want to admit this fact to itself. So we use the sense of well-being that comes with playing and working with the breath to put the mind in a mood where it's much more willing to admit its shortcomings and to do something about them.

• *As you work and play with the breath, you also find that you have strategies for dealing with pain.* Sometimes allowing breath energy to flow right through the pain can help lessen it. At the very least, the pain becomes less of a burden on the mind. This, too, allows you to face the pain with confidence. You're less and less likely to feel overwhelmed by it.

• *Finally, working with the breath in this way shows you the extent to which you shape your present experience*—and how you can learn to shape it more skillfully. As I said above, the mind is primarily active in its approach to experience. Discernment, too, has to be active in understanding where the processes of the mind are skillful and unskillful in the shape they give to things. Discernment doesn't come just from watching passively as things arise and pass away in your experience. It also has to see *why* they arise and *why* they pass away. To do this, it has to experiment—trying to make skillful qualities arise and unskillful qualities pass away—to see which causes are connected to which effects.

In particular, discernment comes from engaging with your present intentions, to see the extent to which those intentions play a role in shaping the way experiences arise and pass away. The Buddhist term for this act of shaping is *fabrication*—in the sense of fabricating a strategy—and fabrication comes in three forms.

— First is *bodily fabrication:* the fabrication of your sense of the body through the in-and-out breath. The way you breathe influences your heart rate, the release of hormones into the blood stream, and the way you experience the body in general.

— Second, there's *verbal fabrication.* This is the way you direct your thoughts to something and evaluate it. These two processes of directed thought and evaluation are the basis of your internal conversation. You bring up topics in the mind to think about, and then make comments on them.

— Third, there's *mental fabrication.* This consists of perceptions and feelings. Perceptions are the labels you put on things: the words by which you name them, or the images the mind associates with them, sending itself subliminal messages about them. Feelings are the feeling-tones of pleasure, pain, or neither-pleasure-nor-pain, which can be either physical or mental.

These three forms of fabrication shape your every experience. Take an example: Your boss has called you into her office for a meeting. As you go to the meeting, you call to mind some of the difficult exchanges you've had with her in the past. This is perception, a form of mental fabrication. You think about the possible issues that might be discussed, and you're concerned that she's going to reprimand you. This is verbal fabrication. As a result of your concerns, your breathing becomes constricted, causing your heart to speed up. This is bodily fabrication. All these forms of fabrication lead to feelings of mental and physical dis-ease, which are another form of mental fabrication. As you open the door to her office, these forms of fabrication already have you primed to overreact to even the slightest expressions of dislike or contempt in her words and bodily language—or to see such expressions even when they're not there.

This is an example in which these three forms of fabrication have you primed to enter into the meeting in a way that will affect not only your experience of the meeting, but also your boss's experience of you. Even before the meeting has started, you're increasing the chances that it won't go well.

But you could also use the power of fabrication to shift the meeting in another direction. Before opening the door, you stop to take a few deep, relaxing breaths (bodily fabrication plus feeling as a mental fabrication), and then call to mind the fact that your boss has been suffering from a lot of stress lately (perception as a mental fabrication). Putting yourself in her shoes, you think of ways in which to approach the meeting in a spirit of cooperation (verbal fabrication). You open the door to a different meeting.

These three forms of fabrication shape not only your external experiences. They're also—and primarily—the processes shaping the different members of the mind's committee, as well as the means by which the different committee members interact. Verbal fabrications are the most obvious way in which these members shout or whisper in one another's ears—your many inner ears—but verbal fabrications are not the only way. For instance, if one of the members is advocating anger, it will also hijack your breathing, making it labored and uncomfortable. This leads you to believe that you've got to get the uncomfortable feeling associated with the anger out of your system by saying or doing something under its influence. Anger will also flash perceptions and images of danger and injustice through your mind, in the same way that devious television producers might flash subliminal messages on your television screen to make you hate and fear the people they don't like.

It's because we're ignorant of the many levels on which these fabrications shape our actions that we suffer from stress. To end that suffering, we have to bring these fabrications into the light of our alertness and discernment.

Working and playing with the breath is an ideal way to do this, because when you work with the breath, you bring all three kinds of fabrication together. You're adjusting and observing the breath; you're thinking about the breath and evaluating the breath; you use the perceptions of the breath to stay with the breath, and you evaluate the feelings that arise when you work with the breath.

This allows you to be more sensitive to the fabrication of what's going on in the present. You begin to see how the mind's committee creates pleasure and pain not only while engaged in meditation, but all of the time. By consciously engaging in this fabrication with knowledge and discernment, you can change the balance of power in the mind. You reclaim your breath, your thoughts, your perceptions and feelings so that they can strengthen the skillful members of the committee, and aren't under the power of the unskillful ones. You can actually create new, even more skillful members of the committee, who help you progress on the path.

In this way, you take one of the problems of the mind—its fragmentation into many different voices, many different selves—and turn it to your advantage. As you develop new skills in meditation, you train new members of the committee who can reason with and convert the more impatient members, showing them how to cooperate in finding a true happiness. As for the members that can't be converted, they gradually lose their power because their promises of happiness are no match for the promises of the new members who actually deliver. So the blatantly unskillful members gradually disappear.

As your practice of concentration and discernment develops, you become more sensitive to the stresses and sufferings caused by fabrication even in activities that you used to regard as pleasant. This makes you become more ardent in looking for a way out. And when discernment sees that the way you fabricate stress and suffering in the present moment is unnecessary, you lose your taste for those fabrications and can let them stop. That's how the mind becomes free.

In the beginning, you gain this freedom step by step, starting from the most blatant levels of fabrication. As the meditation develops, discernment frees you from progressively subtler levels until it can drop the subtlest levels that stand in the way of the unfabricated dimension: the unconditioned dimension that constitutes the ultimate happiness.

Your first taste of this dimension shows you that the most important premise underlying breath meditation is right: An unconditioned happiness is possible. Even though, at this stage, your taste of this dimension doesn't totally put an end to suffering and stress, it does confirm that you're on the right path. You'll be able to reach it for sure. And at that point, you'll have no more need for books of this sort.

Because the breath is so helpful in developing all three aspects of the path to unconditioned happiness—virtue, concentration, and discernment—it's an ideal theme for training the mind to experience that happiness for itself.

*Additional readings:*

(In every case where no author is listed, the writings are mine.)

On the values underlying the practice: "Affirming the Truths of the Heart"; "Karma"; "The Seeds of Karma"; "Generosity First" in *Meditations;* "Purity of Heart"; *The Buddha's Teachings*

On the committee of the mind: *Selves & Not-self;* "The Wisdom of the Ego"

On the suffering that the mind creates for itself: "Life Isn't Just Suffering"; "Ignorance"

On the questions of discernment: "Questions of Skill"
On the four noble truths: "Untangling the Present"; "What's
Noble about the Noble Truths?"; "Truths with Consequences."
For more detail, see *On the Path* and *The Wings to Awakening*.
On the role of moderation and discernment in the practice:
"The Middles of the Middle Way"
On the meaning of mindfulness: "Mindfulness Defined";
"The Agendas of Mindfulness"
On the element of play in the practice: "The Joy of Effort";
"Joy in Effort" in *Meditations 5*
It's good to have a few books of short Dhamma passages that
you can open at random to get a Buddhist perspective on things. In
addition to the traditional *Dhammapada* and *Udana*, I'd recommend:
Ajaan Fuang Jotiko – *Awareness Itself;* Ajaan Lee Dhammadharo –
*The Skill of Release;* Ajaan Dune Atulo – *Gifts He Left Behind;* Ajahn
Chah Subhaddo – *In Simple Terms; It's Like This;* and Upasika Kee
Nanayon – "Pure & Simple" in *An Unentangled Knowing.*

*Relevant talks:*

2007/6/6: The Noble Search for Happiness

2011/10/17: Why Train the Mind

2011/12/22: Countercultural Values

2012/4/4: The Intelligent Heart

2012/6/20: Homeschooling Your Inner Children

2005/3/7: The Open Committee

2011/2/6: Organizing Your Inner Committee

2006/1/13: Unskillful Voices

2005/5/21: Karma of Self & Not-self

2005/4/12: The Need for Stillness

2005/3/27: Everybody Suffers

2004/1/9: Why the Breath

2010/8/13: Why Mindfulness

2009/7/23: Concentration Nurtured with Virtue

2001/5: Concentration & Insight

PART ONE

# *Basic Instructions*

## I : GETTING READY TO MEDITATE

Meditation is something you can do in any situation and in any posture. However, some situations are more conducive than others to helping the mind settle down. Especially when you're just getting started, it's wise to look for situations where there's a minimum of disturbance, both physical and mental.

Also, some postures are more conducive than others to helping the mind settle down. The standard posture for meditation is sitting, and it's wise to learn how to sit in a way that allows you to meditate for long periods of time without moving and without at the same time causing undue pain or harm for the body. Other standard postures for meditating are walking, standing, and lying down. We'll focus here on sitting, and save the other postures for section IV of Part One, below.

Before you sit to meditate on the breath, it's wise to look at three things in this order: your physical situation, your posture, and your mental situation—in other words, the state of your mind.

### YOUR PHYSICAL SITUATION

**Where to meditate.** Choose a quiet spot, in your home or outside. For a daily meditation routine, it's good to choose a spot that you don't normally use for other purposes. Tell yourself that the only thing you're going to do when you sit in that spot is to meditate. You'll begin to develop quiet associations with that spot each time you sit there. It becomes your special place to settle down and be still. To make it even more calming, try to keep the area around it neat and clean.

**When to meditate.** Choose a good time to meditate. Early in the morning, right after you've woken up and washed your face, is often best, for your body is rested and your mind hasn't yet become cluttered with issues from the day. Another good time is in the evening, after you've rested a bit from your daily work. Right before you go to sleep is *not* the best time to meditate, for the mind will keep telling itself, "As soon as this is over, I'm going to bed." You'll start associating meditation with sleep, and, as the Thais say, your head will start looking for the pillow as soon as you close your eyes.

If you have trouble sleeping, then by all means meditate when you're lying in bed, for meditation is a useful substitute for sleep. Often it can be *more* refreshing than sleep, for it can dissolve bodily and mental tensions better than sleeping can. It can also calm you down enough so that worries don't sap your energy or keep you awake. But make sure that you also set aside another time of the day to meditate too, so that you don't always associate meditation with sleep. You want to develop it as an exercise in staying alert.

Also, it's generally not wise to schedule your regular meditation for right after a large meal. Your body will be directing the blood down to your digestive system, and that will tend to make you drowsy.

**Minimizing disturbance.** If you're living with other people, tell them you don't want to be disturbed while you're meditating unless there's a serious emergency. You're taking some time out to be an easier person to live with. If you're the only adult at home, and you're living with children for whom everything is a serious emergency, choose a time when the children are asleep. If you're living with older children, explain to them that you'll be meditating for *x* amount of time and you need privacy during that time. If they interrupt you with a non-emergency, quietly tell them that you're still meditating and that you'll talk with them when you're done. If they want to meditate with you, welcome them, but establish a few rules for their behavior so that they don't disturb your time to be quiet.

Turn off your cell phone and any other devices that might interrupt your meditation.

Use a watch or a clock with a timer to time your meditation. In the beginning, twenty minutes is usually about right, for it gives you enough time to settle down a bit, but not so much time that you start getting bored or frustrated if things aren't going well. As you gain some skill in the meditation, you can gradually increase your meditation time by five- or ten-minute increments.

Once you've set your timer, put it behind you or off to your side so that you can't see it while you're in your meditation position. That will help you to avoid the temptation to peek at the time and to turn your meditation into an exercise in clock-watching.

If you have a dog in your home, put it in another room and close the door. If it starts to whine and scratch at the door, let it into the room where you're sitting, but be strict with yourself in being unresponsive if it comes to you for attention. Most dogs, after a few days, will get the message that when you're sitting there with your eyes closed, you're not going to respond. The dog may well lie down and rest along with you. But if it doesn't get the message, put it back in the other room.

Cats are usually less of a problem in this regard, but if you do have an attention-starved cat, treat it as you would a dog.

### YOUR POSTURE

An important part of training the mind lies in training the body to stay still so that you can focus on the movements of the mind without being disturbed by the movement of the body. If you're not used to sitting still for long periods of time, the act of training the body will have to go along with training the mind.

If you're new to meditation, it's wise not to focus too much on your posture for the first several sessions. That way you can give your full attention to training the mind, saving the process of training the body for when you've had some success in focusing on the breath.

So for beginners, simply sit in a comfortable way, spread thoughts of goodwill—a wish for true happiness—to yourself and others, and then follow the steps in the section, "Focusing on the Breath," below. If your posture gets uncomfortable, you may shift slightly to relieve the discomfort, but try to keep your attention focused on the breath while you shift position.

If, after a while, you feel ready to focus on your posture, here are some things you can try:

**Sitting on the floor.** An ideal posture is to sit cross-legged on the floor, with at most a folded blanket under you—placed just under your sitting bones or under your folded legs as well.

This is a classic meditation posture for at least two good reasons:

One, it's stable. You're not likely to fall over even when, in the more advanced levels of meditation, your sense of the body gets replaced by a sense of space or pure knowing.

Two, when you're accustomed to this posture, you can sit and meditate anywhere. You can go out into the woods, place a small mat on the ground, sit down, and there you are. You don't have to carry a lot of cushions or other paraphernalia around with you.

A standard version of the posture is this:

• Sit on the floor or your folded blanket with your left leg folded in front of you, and your right leg folded on top of your left leg. Place your hands on your lap, palms up, with your right hand on top of the left. (To prevent this posture from causing an imbalance in your spine, you can alternate

sides by sometimes placing your left leg on top of your right leg, and your left hand on top of your right hand.)
• Bring your hands close to your stomach. This will help keep your back straight and minimize the tendency to hunch over.

• Sit straight, look straight in front of you, and close your eyes. If closing your eyes makes you feel uncomfortable or induces feelings of sleepiness, you can leave them half open—although if you do, don't look straight ahead. Lower your gaze to a spot on the floor about three feet in front of you. Keep your focus soft. Be careful not to let it harden into a stare.

• Notice if your body feels like it's leaning to the left or the right. If it is, relax the muscles that are pulling it in that direction, so that you bring your spine into a reasonably straight alignment.

• Pull your shoulders back slightly and then down, to create a slight arch in your middle and lower back. Pull your stomach in a bit, so that the back muscles aren't doing all the work in keeping you erect.

• Relax into this posture. In other words, see how many muscles you can relax in your torso, hips, etc., and still stay erect. This step is important, for it helps you to stay with the posture with a minimum of strain.

This is called the *half-lotus* position, because only one leg is on top of the other. In the *full-lotus*, once your right leg is on top of your left, you bring your left leg on top of your right. This is an extremely stable position if you can manage it, but don't try it until you're adept at the half-lotus.

If you're not accustomed to the half-lotus, you may find in the beginning that your legs will quickly fall asleep. That's because blood that normally flows in the main arteries is being pushed into the small capillaries. This can be uncomfortable at first, but don't worry. You're not harming the body, for the body can adapt. If the small capillaries carry an increased load of blood frequently enough, they will enlarge, and your circulatory system will be rerouted to accommodate your new posture.

The trick with *all* postures is to break yourself in gradually. Pushing yourself to sit long hours right from the start is not wise, for you can damage your knees. If you know any good yoga teachers, ask them to recommend some yoga poses that will help limber up your legs and hips. Do those poses before you meditate to speed up the body's adaptation to the sitting posture.

A somewhat gentler way of sitting cross-legged than the half-lotus is the *tailor* position: Fold your legs, but don't put the right leg on top of the left. Place it on the floor in front of the left, so that your right knee makes a gentler angle, and the left leg isn't pressed down by the right. This helps relieve some of the pressure on both legs.

**Benches & chairs.** If you have a knee or hip injury that makes it difficult to sit cross-legged, you can try sitting on a meditation bench, to see if that's easier. Kneel with your shins on the ground, place the bench over your calves, and then sit back on the bench. Some benches are designed to force you to sit at a certain angle. Others can rock back and forth, allowing you to choose your own angle or to change it at will. Some people like this; others find it unstable. It's a personal choice.

If none of these three alternatives—sitting right on the floor, sitting on the floor on top of a folded blanket, or sitting on a meditation bench—works for you, there are many styles of meditation cushions available for purchase. They're usually a waste of money, though, because an extra folded blanket or firm pillow can usually serve the same purpose. Pillows and blankets may not look as serious as a dedicated meditation cushion, but there's no need to pay a lot of extra money just for looks. A good lesson in becoming a meditator is learning how to improvise with what you've got.

Alternatively, you can try sitting on a chair.

Choose a chair with a seat just high enough off the ground so that your feet can rest flat on the ground and your knees can bend at a ninety-degree angle. A wooden or other firm chair, with or without a folded blanket or thin cushion on the seat, is ideal. Too thick a cushion is unwise, for it leads you to hunch over.

When you've got a good chair, sit slightly away from the back, so that your back supports itself. Then follow the same steps as with the half-lotus: Place your hands on your lap, palms up, one on top of the other. Bring your hands close to your stomach. Sit straight, look straight in front of you, and close your eyes. Pull your shoulders back slightly and then down, to create a nice arch in your middle and lower back. Pull your stomach in a bit. Relax into this posture. In other words, see how many muscles you can relax and still maintain it.

If you're too ill or disabled to sit in any of these postures, choose a posture that feels comfortable for your particular condition.

With any posture, if you discover that you have a tendency over time to slump your back, it may be because of the way you breathe out. Pay a little extra attention to your out-breaths, reminding yourself to keep your back straight each time you breathe out. Keep this up until you've established it as a habit.

And whatever your posture, remember that you don't have to make a vow at the beginning not to move. If you find yourself in extreme pain, wait a minute so that you don't become a slave to every passing pain, and then very consciously—without thinking of anything else—shift your posture to something more comfortable. Then resume your meditation.

### THE STATE OF YOUR MIND

Once your body is in position, take a couple of deep in-and-out breaths, and then look at the state of your mind. Is it staying with the breath, or is a persistent mood getting in the way? If you're staying with the breath, keep going. If some of the members of your mind's committee are less cooperative, bring in some other members to counteract them. The important point is that you don't let a mood dictate whether you're going to meditate or not. Remember, a bad meditation session is better than no meditation session at all. At the very least, you learn to resist the unskillful members of your mind to at least some extent. And only through resisting them can you come to understand them—in the same way that building a dam across a river is a good way to learn how strong the river's currents are.

If some of your committee members are getting in the way, there are some standard contemplations to counteract them. The purpose of these contemplations is to cut through the mind's usual narratives and to create some new committee members with new narratives that will help put things into perspective so that you're more willing to stay with the breath.

**The sublime attitudes.** The most popular contemplation is to develop attitudes of goodwill, compassion, empathetic joy, and equanimity for all beings, without limit. These attitudes—called *brahmaviharas,* or sublime attitudes—are so useful that many people make a standard practice of developing them for a few minutes at the beginning of every meditation session regardless of whether there's a conscious need for them. This helps to clear up any buried resentments from your daily interactions with other people, and reminds you of why you're meditating: You want to find a happiness that's secure—which means that it has to be harmless. Meditation is one of the few ways of finding happiness that harms no one at all. At the same time, you're creating a new narrative for your life: Instead of being a person weighed down by resentments, you show yourself that you can rise above difficult situations and develop a magnanimous heart.

The four sublime attitudes are actually contained in two: goodwill and equanimity. Goodwill is a wish for true happiness, both for yourself and for all others. Compassion is the attitude that goodwill develops when it sees people suffering or acting in ways that will lead to suffering. You want them to stop suffering. Empathetic joy is the attitude that goodwill develops when it sees people happy or acting in ways that will lead to happiness. You want them to continue being happy. Equanimity is the attitude you have to develop when you realize that certain things are beyond your control. If you let yourself get worked up over them, you waste the energy you could have applied to areas where you *can* have an effect. So you try to put your mind on an even keel toward the things you can't control, beyond the sway of your likes and dislikes.

*Here's an exercise for developing goodwill and equanimity:*

Remind yourself of what goodwill is—a wish for true happiness—and that, in spreading thoughts of goodwill, you're wishing that you and all others will develop the *causes* for true happiness. You're also establishing the intention to further true happiness in any way you can, within your own mind and in your dealings with others. Of course, not everyone will act in line with your wish, which is why it's important also to develop thoughts of equanimity to cover the cases where people refuse to act in the interests of true happiness. That way you won't suffer so much when people act unskillfully, and you can stay focused on the cases where you *can* be of help.

For goodwill, begin by stating in your mind a traditional expression of goodwill for yourself: *"May I be happy. May I be free from stress and pain. May I be free from animosity, free from trouble, free from oppression. May I look after myself with ease."*

Then spread similar thoughts to others, in ever-widening circles: people close to your heart, people you like, people you're neutral about, people you don't like, people you don't even know—and not just people: all living beings in all directions. In each case, say to yourself, *"May you be happy. May you be free from stress and pain. May you be free from animosity, free from trouble, free from oppression. May you look after yourself with ease.*" Think of this wish as spreading out in all directions, out to infinity. It helps to enlarge the mind.

To make this a heart-changing practice, ask yourself—when you're secure in your goodwill for yourself—if there's anyone for whom you can't sincerely spread thoughts of goodwill. If a particular person comes to mind, ask yourself: "What would be gained by this person's suffering?" Most of the cruelty in the world comes from people who are suffering and fearful. Only rarely do people who've been acting unskillfully react skillfully to their suffering and change their ways. All too often they do just the opposite: They hunger to make others suffer even more. So the world would be a better place if we could all simply follow the path to true happiness by being generous and virtuous, and by training the mind.

With these thoughts in mind, see if you can express goodwill for this sort of person: "*May you learn the error of your ways, learn the way to true happiness, and look after yourself with ease.*" In expressing this thought, you're not necessarily wishing to love or have continued relations with this person. You're simply making the determination not to seek revenge against those who have acted harmfully, or those whom you have harmed. This is a gift both to yourself and to those around you.

Conclude the session by developing an attitude of equanimity. Remind yourself that all beings will experience happiness or sorrow in line with their actions. In many cases, their actions lie beyond your control, and your own past actions can't be erased. In cases where these actions place obstacles in the way of the happiness you wish for all beings, you simply have to accept the fact with equanimity. That way you can focus on areas where you can make a difference through your present actions. This is why the traditional formula for equanimity focuses on the issue of action:

*"All living beings are the owners of their actions, heir to their actions, born of their actions, are related through their actions, and live dependent on their actions. Whatever they do, for good or for evil, to that will they fall heir."*

Thinking in this way helps you not to get worked up about what you can't change, so that you can devote the energy of your goodwill to what you can.

If there are people for whom goodwill is simply too difficult for you to manage right now, you might try developing thoughts of compassion instead. Think of the ways that *they* may be suffering, to see if that softens your attitude toward them, or helps you understand why they act the way they do. If this is too difficult, you can go straight to thoughts of equanimity about them. In other words, you can remind yourself that you don't have to settle accounts. You're better off freeing yourself from the circle of revenge. The principle of action and its results will take care of the situation.

Just that thought can give the mind some space to settle down and develop some concentration.

By spreading thoughts of goodwill and equanimity to all beings, you take your mind out of its everyday narratives and create a broader perspective for your meditation. It's easiest to settle the mind into the present moment, right here and now, when you've let it think for a few moments about the universe as a whole. When you remember that all beings are looking for happiness—sometimes skillfully, more often not—it puts your own quest for happiness in perspective. You want to do it right.

There are other contemplations to counteract specific unskillful moods that might get in the way of your meditation, such as contemplation of your own acts of generosity and virtue for when you're feeling low self-esteem, contemplation of death for when you're lazy, or contemplation of the unattractive parts of the body for when you're overcome with lust. A few of these contemplations are described in more detail in the Appendix.

## II : FOCUSING ON THE BREATH

Now you're ready to focus on the breath. There are six steps:

*1. Find a comfortable way of breathing.*

Start by taking a couple of deep, long in-and-out breaths. This helps to energize the body for meditation and makes the breath easier to observe. Deep breathing at the beginning of meditation is also a good habit to maintain even as you become more skilled in the practice, for it helps to counteract any tendency to suppress the breath as you try to make the mind still.

Notice where you feel the sensations of breathing in the body: the sensations that tell you, "Now you're taking an in-breath. Now you're taking an out-breath." Notice if they're comfortable. If they are, keep breathing in that way. If they're not, adjust the breath so that it's more comfortable. You can do this in any of three ways:

a. As you continue breathing deep and long, notice where a sense of strain develops in the body toward the end of the in-breath, or where there's a sense of squeezing the breath out toward the end of the out-breath. Ask yourself if you can relax those sensations with the next breath as you maintain the same breathing rhythm. In other words, can you maintain a sense of relaxation in the areas that have been feeling strained toward the end of the in-breath? Can you breathe out at the same rate without squeezing it out? If you can, keep up that rhythm of breathing.

b. Try changing the rhythm and texture of the breath. Experiment with different ways of breathing to see how they feel. You can make the breath shorter or longer. You can try short in and long out, or long in and short out. You can try faster breathing or slower breathing. Deeper or more shallow. Heavier or lighter. Broader or more narrow. When you find a rhythm that feels good, stick with it as long as it feels good. If, after a while, it doesn't feel good, you can adjust the breath again.

c. Simply pose the question in the mind each time you breathe in: "What kind of breath would feel especially gratifying right now?" See how your body responds.

*2. Stay with each in-and-out breath.*

If your attention slips off to something else, bring it right back to the breath. If it wanders off again, bring it back again. If it wanders off 100 times, bring it back 100 times. Don't get discouraged. Don't get upset with yourself. Each time you come back, reward yourself with an especially gratifying breath. That way the mind will develop positive associations with the breath. You'll find it easier to stay with the breath, and to return to it quickly the next time you slip off.

If you get discouraged thinking about how many breaths you're going to have to stay focused on, tell yourself with each breath: "Just this one in-breath; just this one out-breath." The task of staying with the breath will then seem less overwhelming, and your thoughts will be more precisely focused on the present.

If you want, you can use a meditation word to help fasten your attention to the breath. *Buddho* ("awake") is a popular one. Think *bud* with the in-breath, and *dho* with the out. Or you can simply think *in* and *out*. Keep the meditation word as long as the breath. When you find that you can stay easily with the breath, drop the meditation word so that you can observe the breath more clearly.

*3. When the blatant sensations of breathing are comfortable, expand your awareness to different parts of the body to observe more subtle breathing sensations.*

You can do this section-by-section, in any order you like, but in the beginning try to be systematic so that you cover the entire body. Later, when your sensitivity to the body becomes more automatic, you will quickly sense which parts of the body need most attention, and you can direct your attention immediately there. But when you're starting out, it's good to have a clear and comprehensive roadmap in mind.

One roadmap is this:

• Start with the area around the navel. Locate that part of the body in your awareness and watch it for a while as you breathe in and breathe out. See what rhythm and texture of breathing feels best right there. If you notice any sense of tension or tightness in that part of the body, allow it to relax, so that no tension builds up as you breathe in, and you don't hold on to any tension as you breathe out. If you want, you can think of breath energy entering the body right there at the navel, so that you don't create a sense of strain by trying to pull it there from somewhere else. Have a sense that the breath energy is coming in and out freely and easily. There's nothing obstructing it.

• When that part of the body feels refreshed, move your attention to different parts of the front of your torso and repeat the same steps. Survey the parts in this order: the lower right-hand corner of the abdomen, the lower left-hand corner of the abdomen; the solar plexus (the spot right in front of your stomach), the right flank (the side of the rib cage), the left flank; the middle of the chest, the spot to the right of that where the chest and the shoulder meet, the same spot on the left. In other words, you move up the front of the torso, focusing first on the center, then on the right, then on the left. Then you move further up the torso and repeat the same pattern.

• You may find, as you focus on the different parts of the body, that the rhythm and texture of the breathing will change to suit that part of the body. This is perfectly fine.

• Then move your attention to the base of the throat and follow the same steps as for the navel.

• Then bring your attention to the middle of the head. As you breathe in and out, think of the breath energy coming in and out not only through the nose, but also through the eyes, the ears, the back of the neck, the top of the head. Think of the energy gently working through any patterns of tension you may feel in the head—in the jaws, around the eyes, in the forehead—and very gently dissolving those patterns of tension away. When the patterns of tension feel relaxed, you can think of the breath energy going deep into the area around the pineal gland, right behind the eyes, and allowing that part of the body to absorb all the incoming breath energy it needs. But be careful not to put too much pressure on the head, because the nerves of the head tend to be overworked. Apply just enough pressure to maintain your focus comfortably.

• Now move your attention to the back of the neck, right at the base of the skull. As you breathe in, think of the breath energy entering the body at that spot and then going down the shoulders, down the arms, out to the tips of the fingers. As you breathe out, think of the energy radiating out from those parts of the body into the air. As you become more sensitive to these parts of the body, notice which side is carrying more tension: the left shoulder or the right shoulder, the left upper arm or the right upper arm, and so on. Whichever side is holding more tension, consciously try to relax that side and keep it relaxed all the way through the in-breath, all the way through the out-breath.

If you tend to hold a lot of tension in your hands, spend a fair amount of time releasing the tension along the back of each hand and in each finger.

• Now, keeping your focus at the back of the neck, breathe in with the thought that the energy is going down both sides of the spine down to the tailbone. Repeat the same steps as for the shoulders and arms. In other words, when you breathe out, think of the breath energy radiating out from the back into the air. As you become more sensitive to the back, notice which side is carrying more tension and consciously try to keep that side relaxed all the way through the in-breath, all the way through the out-breath.

• Now move your attention down to the tailbone. As you breathe in, think of the breath energy entering the body there, going down past the hips, down the legs, and out to the tips of the toes. Repeat the same steps as for the shoulders and arms. If necessary, you can spend a fair amount of time releasing the tension in your feet and toes.

• That completes one cycle in the survey of the body. If you like, you can go through the body again, beginning at the navel, to see if you can clear up any patterns of tension you may have missed the first time around. You can keep this up as many times as you like until you feel ready to settle down.

The amount of time you spend with each section of the body is up to you. In the beginning, as a general rule of thumb, you might want to spend just a few minutes with each point or section, giving more time to the points on the central meridian of the body than to the points on the side, and even more time to the shoulders, back, and legs. As you become more familiar with the energy patterns in your own body, you can adjust the time spent on each point as you see fit. If one point or section seems to respond especially well to your attention, releasing tension in a refreshing way, stick with that point as long as it responds. If a point or section doesn't respond after several minutes of attention—or if you find that tension increases when you focus on it—drop it for the time being and move on to the next point.

If your time for meditation is limited, you might want to limit your survey to the center points on the front of the torso—navel, solar plexus, middle of the chest—and then to the base of the throat and the middle of the head.

If focusing in the head gives you a headache, avoid focusing there until you learn how to maintain focus with a minimum of pressure.

*4. Choose a spot to settle down.*

You can choose any spot you like where the breath energy is clear and you find it easy to stay focused. A few of the traditional spots are:

a. the tip of the nose,
b. the point between the eyebrows,
c. the middle of the forehead,
d. the top of the head,
e. the middle of the head,
f. the palate,
g. the back of the neck at the base of the skull,
h. the base of the throat,
i. the breastbone (the tip of the sternum),
j. the navel (or a point just above it),
k. the base of the spine.

Over the course of several meditations, you can experiment with different spots to see which ones give the best results. You may also find that other spots not mentioned on this list are also congenial. Or you may find that keeping track of two spots at once—say, the middle of the head and the base of the spine—helps to keep your attention fixed more firmly than focusing just on one spot. Ultimately, you want to be able to keep your attention focused on any spot in the body. This ability will be useful when you're suffering from a disease or injury, as you can sometimes speed healing by focusing on the breath energy at particular spots in the body.

*5. Spread your awareness from that spot so that it fills the body through every in-and-out breath.*

Think of a lit candle in the middle of an otherwise dark room. The flame of the candle is in one spot, but its light fills the entire room. You want your awareness to be centered but broad in just the same way. Your sense of awareness may have a tendency to shrink—especially as you breathe out—so remind yourself with every breath: "whole body breathing in, whole body breathing out." This full-body awareness helps to keep you from getting drowsy when the breath gets comfortable, and from losing focus as the breath gets more subtle.

*6. Think of the breath energy coursing through the whole body with every in-and-out breath.*

Let the breath find whatever rhythm or texture feels best. Think of all the breath energies connecting with one another and flowing in harmony. The more fully they're connected, the more effortless your breathing will be. If you have a sense that the breath-channels are open during the in-breath but close during the out-breath, adjust your perception to keep them open throughout the breathing cycle.

Then simply maintain that sense of whole-body breathing throughout the remainder of your meditation. If the breath grows still, don't worry. The body will breathe if it needs to. When the mind is still, the brain uses less oxygen, so the oxygen that the body receives passively—through the lungs and perhaps through the relaxed pores (anatomists have differing opinions on this)—will be enough to serve its needs. At the same time, however, don't force the breath to stop. Let it follow its own rhythm. Your duty is simply to maintain a broad, centered awareness and to allow the breath to flow freely throughout the body.

If you find that you lose focus when you spread your awareness through the body, you can return to the survey of the

different parts, try a meditation word, or simply stay focused on
one point until you feel ready to try full-body awareness again.

**Variations.** As you get more familiar with the meditation and
with the problems you encounter while doing it, you can adjust
these steps as you see fit. In fact, gaining a sense of how to adjust
things—to learn from your own experimentation—is an important principle in using breath meditation to develop discernment.
For example, you may want to *change the order of the steps*. You
might find that you can more easily find a comfortable way of
breathing (step one) if you first develop a full-body awareness (step
five). Or you might find that you need to force the mind to settle
down firmly in a single spot for a while (step four) before you can
explore the breath sensations in the rest of the body (step three).
You might find that after you've chosen one spot to stay settled in
(step four), you want to focus on two spots at once for a while
before you move on to spreading your awareness to the whole
body (step five).

Another way of adjusting the steps is to *vary what you do within
a particular step*. Step three—exploring the subtle breath sensations
in the body—allows for an especially wide range of variation. You
might want to start your survey at the back of the neck, thinking
of the breath energy entering the body there from the back and
then going down through the spine, and ultimately out the legs to
the tips of the toes and the spaces between the toes. Then think of
the breath coming in the back of the neck going down through the
shoulders and out through the arms to the fingers and the spaces
between the fingers. Then move your attention to the breath sensations in the front of the torso.

Or you might want to go through the body very quickly at
first, and then repeat the survey more methodically.

Or you might visualize changing the direction of how the
breath sensations flow through the body. For instance, instead of

thinking of the breath flowing down the spine and out the feet, you might think of it coming up from the feet, going up the spine, and then either going out the top of the head or over the top of the head and down through your throat and out the area in front of the heart.

Or you might sense that there are breath energies surrounding the body like a cocoon. When this happens, try to get a sense of how to tell when these energies are in harmony, when they're in conflict, and how to bring them from conflict to harmony in a way that nourishes the energies inside the body. One way of doing this is to visualize these energies as all flowing in one direction— say, from the head to the toes—and then, after a while, visualizing them all flowing in the other direction. Notice which direction feels more comfortable, and then stick with that. If the cocoon of breath energies feels comfortable, you can experiment with ways of using that comfortable energy to heal parts of the body that feel tight or in pain.

Another way of adjusting the steps, on certain occasions, is to *focus on only a few of the steps.* There are two main situations in which you might want to try this:

- *When you're first getting started* and you find that the more broadly focused steps—3, 5, and 6—are hard to follow without getting distracted, you can skip them for the time being and focus first on the more narrowly focused steps—1, 2, and 4—until you can stay with them consistently. Only then should you expand your practice to include the other three. However many sessions of meditation this may take doesn't matter. What matters is that you're able to maintain a comfortable center. That will help you add the remaining steps with a greater sense of stability.

- *When you're skilled at combining all six steps* and you want to gain practice in bringing the mind to stillness as quickly as possible, you can focus on steps 4, 5, and 6. In other words, once you've learned from experience where your mind feels most comfortably centered, try settling down quickly in that spot, allow it to get comfortable, and then see how quickly you can spread your awareness along with the comfortable breath to fill the entire body and then keep it filled. This is a useful skill to develop, not only in the context of formal meditation, but also in daily life. This point will be discussed further in Part Three.

These are just a few of the ways you might want to experiment. In general, though, it's usually best to begin with the six steps, in order, so as to have a clear roadmap in mind each time you sit down to meditate. That way, when you've wandered off, you'll find it easier to pick up where you left off. And if a particular stage in the practice goes especially well, you'll be better able to remember it because you know where it is on the map.

## III : LEAVING MEDITATION

There are three steps to leaving meditation skillfully.

*1. Reflect on how your meditation went.*

The purpose here is to pick up useful points for the next time you meditate. Was there any time during the past session that the mind felt especially calm and centered? If there was, ask yourself, "Where were you focused? What was the quality of your focus? What was the quality of your breath? What did you do leading up to that point in your meditation?" Try to remember these things for the next session. You may find that you can re-create that sensation of calm just by repeating the same steps. If you can't, put that memory aside and focus totally on what you're doing in the present. Try to be more observant of these things the next time. It's through being observant that the meditation develops as a skill and gives more reliable results. It's like being a good cook: If you notice which foods please the people you're cooking for, you give them more of the same, and eventually you'll get a bonus or a raise in pay.

*2. Spread thoughts of goodwill again.*

Think of whatever peace and calm you felt for the past session, and dedicate it to other beings: either specific people you know who are suffering right now, or all living beings in all directions—all our companions in birth, aging, illness, and death. May we all find peace and well-being in our hearts.

*3. Try to stay sensitive to the breath energy in the body as you open your eyes and leave the meditation posture.*

Don't let your awareness of the visual field crowd out your awareness of the body-field. And don't let your concern for your next activity cause you to drop your awareness of the breath energy in the body. Try to maintain that sense of full-body awareness as consistently as you can. You may not be able to keep track of the in-and-out breath as you engage in other activities, but you can maintain an overall sense of the quality of breath energy throughout the body. Keep it relaxed and flowing. Notice when you lose your awareness of it; notice how you can regain it. Try to keep the sense of awareness of the breath energy in the body as constant as you can until the next time you sit down to meditate. This way you maintain a solid, nourishing foundation for the mind as you go through the day. This gives you a sense of groundedness. That groundedness provides not only a sense of security and inner ease, but also a basis for observing the movements of the mind. This is one of the ways in which steady mindfulness and alertness form a foundation for insight.

In other words, the most skillful way to leave meditation is not to leave it entirely. Keep it going as much and as long as you can.

## IV : MEDITATING IN OTHER POSTURES

### WALKING MEDITATION

Walking meditation is a good transition between maintaining a still mind when the body is still, and maintaining a still mind in the midst of all your activities. As you walk in a meditative way, you gain practice in protecting the stillness of the mind in the midst of the motion of the body, while at the same time dealing with the fewest possible outside distractions.

An ideal time to practice walking meditation is right after you've been doing sitting meditation, so that you can bring a mind already stilled, to at least some extent, to the practice. Some people, though, find that the mind settles down more quickly while sitting if they've done a session of walking meditation first. This is a matter of personal temperament.

If you're meditating right after a meal, it's wise to do walking meditation rather than sitting meditation, for the motion of the body helps both to digest your food and to ward off drowsiness.

There are two ways of practicing walking meditation: walking back and forth on a set path, and going for a stroll. The first way is more conducive for helping the mind to settle down; the second is more convenient when you don't have access to an undisturbed path where you can walk back and forth without rousing curiosity or concerns from other people.

1. **Walking on a path.** Choose a level path anywhere from 20 to 70 paces long. Ideally, it should be a straight path, but if you can't find a straight path that long, try an L-shaped or a U-shaped path. If you're going to time your meditation, set the timer and put it someplace near the path but facing away so that you won't be able to see how much time is left while you're walking.

Stand at one end of the path for a moment. Gently clasp one hand with the other, either in front of you or behind you, and let your arms hang down comfortably. If you have your hands in front of you, have both palms facing your body. If behind you, have both palms facing away from your body. Close your eyes and check to see if your body feels properly aligned, leaning neither to the left nor to the right. If it feels out of alignment, relax the muscles that are pulling it out of alignment, so that your body is as balanced as possible.

Bring your attention to the breath. Take a couple of long, deep in-and-out breaths, and focus your attention on the breath sensations in one part of the body. It's usually wise, in the beginning, to choose a point anywhere on a line drawn down the middle of the front of your torso. If you focus in your head, you tend to stay in your head: You don't get a clear sense of the body walking, and it's easy to slip off into thoughts of the past and future. If you focus on a point on one side of the body, it can pull you out of balance.

However, if in the beginning you find it hard to keep track of a still point in the torso, you can simply stay aware of the movement of your legs or feet, or of the sensations in your hands. As your mind settles down, you can then try finding a comfortable place in the torso.

Breathe in a way that allows the spot you've chosen to feel comfortable, open, and refreshed.

Open your eyes and gaze either straight ahead of you, or down at the path several paces in front of you, but don't let your head tilt forward. Keep it straight.

Make sure that you're still clearly aware of the point of your internal focus on the breath, and then start walking. Walk at a normal pace, or slightly slower than normal. Don't gaze around while you walk. Maintain your inner attention at your chosen point in the body all along the path. Allow the breath to find a comfortable rhythm. There's no need to breathe in sync with your steps.

When you reach the other end of the path, stop for a moment to make sure that your attention is still with your chosen point. If it's wandered off, bring it back. Then turn to face in the opposite direction and walk back to where you started, maintaining focus on your chosen point. Stop at that end of the path for a moment again, to make sure that your attention is still with your chosen point. Then turn to face in the opposite direction and walk back again. If you find it helpful in calming the mind, you can decide beforehand to turn either clockwise or counter-clockwise each time you turn.

Repeat these steps until your predetermined time is over.

In the beginning it's best to focus on maintaining your attention at your one chosen point in the body as much as you can, as you would in step 4 of the sitting meditation. This is because you're balancing attention to several things at once: your chosen point, the fact that you're walking, and the fact that you have to be aware enough of your surroundings so that you don't stray off the path, walk past the designated end, or bump into anything. That's enough to keep you fully occupied at first.

As you get more proficient at this, you can start paying more attention to how the breath energies flow in the different parts of your body as you walk—while at the same time maintaining the primary focus at your chosen point—in much the same way that you maintain a centered but broad awareness in step 5 of the sitting meditation. You can make a game of seeing how quickly you can move from being focused comfortably on one spot to spreading your awareness and the sense of comfort throughout the body. Once it's spread, see how long you can keep it that way as you continue walking. As we'll see in Part Three, this is an important skill to develop to maintain a sense of secure well-being throughout daily life.

Some people find that their minds can gather into strong concentration while walking. But generally, you'll find that you can get into deeper concentration while sitting than while walking, because you have more things to keep track of while you're walking. However, the fact that your attention has to move between three things when you're walking—your still point, the motion of your walking, and an awareness of your surroundings—means that you get to see clearly the movements of the mind in a restricted field. This provides a good opportunity for observing them carefully and for gaining insight into their various ways of deceiving you.

For instance, you'll come to notice how unbidden thoughts try to take advantage of the fact that the mind is moving quickly among three things. These thoughts slip into that movement and hijack it, directing it away from your meditation. As soon as you notice this happening, stop walking for a moment, return your attention to your chosen spot, and then resume walking. Ultimately you'll see the movement of those unbidden thoughts but won't move along with them. When you don't move with them, they go for just a little way and then disappear. This is an important skill in gaining insight into the workings of the mind.

**2. Going for a stroll.** If you're going to practice walking meditation by going for a stroll, you have to lay down a few rules for yourself so that it doesn't turn into just an ordinary stroll.

Choose an area that's relatively quiet and where you won't run into people who will want you to stop and chat with them. A park is good, as is a quiet, backcountry lane. If you're walking around your neighborhood, go in a direction you don't normally go and where the neighbors won't try to engage you in conversations. If someone does call out to you, make it a rule that you'll nod and smile in response, but won't say any more words than are necessary.

Before you start your walk, stand for a moment to put your body in alignment, and bring your attention to your chosen spot for observing the breath. Breathe in a way that keeps that spot comfortable and refreshed. Think of it as a bowl filled to the brim with water, and you don't want to spill a drop. Walk at a normal pace in a manner that's composed but doesn't look unnatural. You want to keep your secret: that you're doing walking meditation and you don't want anyone else to know. Gaze around only as much as is necessary and appropriate to keep yourself safe. If your thoughts start wandering off, stop for a moment and reestablish your primary focus at your chosen point. Take a couple of especially refreshing breaths, and then resume walking. If people are around, and you don't want to call attention to yourself, pretend that you're looking at something to the side of your path while reestablishing your focus.

Whether you practice walking meditation on a set path or as a stroll, conclude the session by standing still for a moment and following the three steps for leaving meditation, as discussed under section III, above.

## STANDING MEDITATION

Standing meditation is rarely done on its own. It's more often done as a part of walking meditation. It's especially good for five situations while you're walking:

1. When your thoughts slip away from the breath, stop and stand for a moment until you can reestablish your focus at your chosen point. Then resume walking. If your mind is especially restless, you may want to stand for a while. In this case, take advantage of the fact that you're standing still, close your eyes, and see if the body feels aligned. If you're slouching, straighten up, pull in your stomach a bit, pull your shoulders back and then down a bit, to create a slight arch in your back. If you're leaning to one side or the other, relax whichever muscles are pulling you

out of alignment. Then relax into this straightened posture so that you can maintain it with a minimum of strain.

2. When the walking has you fatigued but you aren't yet ready to stop walking meditation, stand for a few minutes to rest, paying attention to your posture as in step 1.

3. When you're trying to master the skill of spreading your awareness, along with the comfortable breath, from one spot to fill the entire body, you might find it easier to do this while you're standing still. Once it's spread, resume walking. If you lose that sense of the entire body, stop and stand still so that you can recover it more easily.

4. When the mind, in spite of the movement of the body, gathers into a strong sense of concentration, stop and stand still to allow it to gather fully. Some meditators arrange a place next to their meditation path where they can sit down if the mind gathers so strongly that even standing still is a distraction.

5. When an interesting insight into the mind comes to you while you're walking, stop and stand so that you can observe it more carefully. In cases like this, you may not want to devote too much attention to your posture, as that might distract you from what you're observing in the mind.

As a general rule, while standing, keep your hands clasped in front of you or behind you as you would when walking.

## MEDITATION LYING DOWN

To meditate while lying down is very conducive for attaining strong concentration. Some people find that it's actually more conducive for concentration than the sitting posture.

However, it's also conducive for falling asleep. This is why your main concern when meditating while lying down is to stay awake.

It's generally better to meditate while lying on your right side, rather than on your left side, on your back, or on your stomach. If you have to lie down for long periods of time—as when you're ill—there's nothing wrong with shifting your posture among these four lying postures and meditating all the while.

However, lying on the right side has three advantages. First is that the heart is above the head, which improves the blood flow to the brain. (This means that if your physiology is reversed, with the heart on your right side, you'd do better to meditate while lying on your left side.) Second, it's better for digestion. Third—and here lying on the right side shares this point with lying on the left—you can make a point of placing one foot on top of the other and keeping it there, not allowing it to slip off. The amount of attention this requires you to devote to your feet can help keep you awake.

Have your head supported with a pillow at the proper height for keeping your spine relatively straight. If you're lying on your right side, place your right arm slightly in front of you so that the body doesn't weigh on it. Fold your arm so that your right hand is lying palm-up in front of your face. Allow your left arm to lie straight along the body, with your left palm facing down.

The steps for surveying your mind, focusing on the breath, and leaving meditation are the same as for sitting meditation.

## V : BECOMING A MEDITATOR

Meditating is one thing. Becoming a meditator is something else. It means developing a set of inner identities around the activities of meditation. Ideally, as you meditate, these identities should take on growing influence within your inner committee.

The activities around which these identities grow are the three needed for concentration: mindfulness, alertness, and ardency. When you focus on the breath in line with the above instructions, mindfulness is what keeps the instructions in mind, alertness is what watches what you're doing and the results that come from what you're doing, while ardency is what tries to do it well. When you slip off the breath, ardency tries to come right back to the breath as quickly as possible. While you're with the breath, ardency tries to be as sensitive as possible to what's going well and what isn't. When things aren't going well, it tries to figure out why, so that it can improve them. When they are going well, it tries to maintain them so that they can grow.

As these qualities get stronger with practice, they begin to coalesce into two distinct identities, two new members of your mind's committee. The more passive of the two is *the observer*, which develops around alertness. This is the part of the mind that steps back a bit and simply watches what's going on with a minimum of interference. As it develops, it gives you practice in exercising your patient endurance—your ability to stick with things even when they're unpleasant—and in exercising your equanimity, your ability not to react to things, so that you can see them clearly for what they are.

The more active of the two identities is *the doer*, which develops around mindfulness and ardency. This is the part that tries to make things go well; that, when they aren't going well, asks questions and investigates to understand why, tries to remember what worked in the past, and then decides how to respond—when it's best to interfere and when it's not. When things *are* going well, this identity tries to keep them going well. Over the course of time, you'll find that the doer can assume many roles, such as the investigator and the director. This part exercises your ingenuity and imagination, as you try to shape things in the best possible direction.

These two identities help each other along. The observer provides the doer with accurate information on which to base its decisions so that it doesn't simply try to force its will on things and deny when it's done harm. The doer does its best to make sure that the observer doesn't lose balance and start providing biased information—as when it's tempted to stay focused on one side of an issue and to ignore another side. Sometimes the back-and-forth between these two identities is fairly quick. At other times—especially when you can't figure something out and simply have to watch what's going on—you'll find yourself identifying with the observer for a fairly long time before gaining enough information to pass on to the doer.

A large part of the skill in meditating is learning *when* to assume these identities while you practice. They're especially helpful in dealing with problems in the mind, as we'll see in Part Two. When you're faced with pain, for instance, they provide you with alternative identities that you can assume in relation to the pain. Instead of having to be the victim of the pain, you can be the observer of the pain. Or you can take on the role of the investigator, trying to figure out what the pain is and why the mind is turning it into a burden.

Similarly, when an unskillful emotion comes into the mind, you don't have to identify yourself as the person who feels the emotion or agrees with it. You can be the observer, stepping back from the emotion. Or, as the doer, you can be the investigator, taking the emotion apart; or the director, assembling a new emotion to replace it.

As your concentration strengthens, the observer and doer will continue to be helpful. On the level of strong concentration called jhana (see Part Four), they turn into a factor called *evaluation:* the discernment factor that helps to settle the mind down through understanding its needs and providing for them. The observer acts as the passive side of evaluation, the doer acts as the active side. Working together, they can take you far in the practice.

So even though these members of your committee are forms of becoming, they're useful forms. Don't throw them away until you reach the point where they have no more help to offer. In the meantime, get to know them by exercising them. Because your mind's committee has a lot of unskillful members, you'll need all the inner help you can get.

*Additional readings:*

On meditation as a skill: "The Joy of Effort"; "Joy in Effort" in *Meditations5;* "Strength Training for the Mind"; "Adolescent Practice" in *Meditations2*
A talk by Ajaan Lee Dhammadharo—"Observe & Evaluate" in *Inner Strength*—also gives a good perspective on meditation as a skill.
On the role of desire and imagination in the practice: "Pushing the Limits"
On the relationship between mindfulness and concentration: "The Path of Mindfulness & Concentration"
For more advanced discussions of mindfulness and concentration: *Right Mindfulness; On the Path;* Ajaan Lee Dhammadharo – *Frames of Reference*
On breath meditation: Ajaan Lee Dhammadharo, *Keeping the Breath in Mind,* in particular "Method 2." Ajaan Lee's talks in *Lessons in Samadhi* are very useful for getting a fuller perspective on his approach to breath meditation, as are the talks in the section of *Inner Strength* entitled, "Inner Skill." The short fragments in the sections of *The Skill of Release* entitled "Beginning Concentration," "The Basics of Breathing," and "All-around Discernment" offer useful tips.
For more useful tips, see the sections of Ajaan Fuang Jotiko – *Awareness Itself* entitled, "Meditation," "Breathing," "Visions & Signs," and "Right at Awareness"
On the brahmaviharas: *The Sublime Attitudes;* "Head & Heart Together"; "Metta Means Goodwill"; "The Limitations of the Unlimited Attitudes"
On walking meditation: "Walking Meditation: Stillness in Motion" in *Meditations4*
For short talks to read before you meditate: any of the books in the *Meditations* series

*Relevant talks:*

2012/2/4: IN SHAPE TO MEDITATE
2004/7/24: MAINTAINING GOODWILL
2005/9/2: METTA MEDITATION
2011/12/21: GOODWILL & HEEDFULNESS
The collection of talks entitled *Basics* contains many talks dealing with issues that arise as you start learning how to focus on the breath.
2011/8/10: GATHER 'ROUND THE BREATH
2006/11/3: ALLOWING THE BREATH TO SPREAD
2010/2/7: BRAHMAVIHARAS AT THE BREATH
2011/12/5: TURN OFF THE AUTOMATIC PILOT
2012/7/21: CHOICEFUL AWARENESS
2011/8/16: ARTILLERY ALL AROUND
2011/12/6: VIEWS, VIRTUE, & MINDFULNESS
2005/4/22: EKAGGATA
2011/4/10: TRAINING YOUR MINDS
2011/9/27: EQUANIMITY
2012/1/21: A MIRROR FOR THE MIND
2007/5/8: CENTERED IN THE BODY
2010/3/28: MINDFUL JUDGMENT

PART TWO

# Common Problems

Everyone encounters problems and difficult patches in the course of meditating, so don't let them get you upset. Don't view them as signs that you're making no progress or that you're a hopeless meditator. Problems are an excellent opportunity for figuring out where you have unskillful habits and learning how to do something about them. This is what develops your discernment. In fact, the process of learning how to deal with the two most common problems in meditation, pain and wandering thoughts, is what has brought many people in the past to awakening.

The strategies offered here in Part Two focus on what you might do to deal with these problems *while you're meditating*. If you find that they don't work for you, try improvising some solutions on your own. This is how you develop your own personal tool kit as a meditator, so that you have a wide range of strategies for dealing with problems as they occur. If you stick to only one strategy, the anti-meditation factions of your committee will quickly find ways to work around that strategy. If you can vary your strategies, you're not such an easy mark for their ploys.

If nothing you do while meditating seems to work, the real problem may lie in the way you live your life as a whole. Suggestions for how you might adjust your life to support your meditation are given in Part Three.

## PAIN

Pain is something you will encounter, on and off, throughout the course of meditation, so you have to learn to view it with discernment and equanimity, as something perfectly normal. Again, don't let yourself get upset around the pain. You might find it useful to drop the word "pain," and replace it with "pains," for not all pains are alike. Learning the differences among them is one of the prime ways you'll develop discernment into the workings of the mind.

If the pains you encounter while sitting in meditation are connected to an old injury, surgery, or structural imbalance, adjust your posture so as not to aggravate your condition. For instance, if you're trying to sit cross-legged but have an injured knee, you might place a folded blanket or small pillow under the knee to help support it. If this doesn't help, sit in a chair.

A good rule of thumb is that if the pain disappears a few minutes after getting up from meditation, you know you aren't harming your body.

If, as you're just getting started in the meditation, the pain makes it impossible to keep focused on the breath, tell yourself that you'll sit with it for a few minutes so that you don't get into the habit of jumping every time it cracks the whip, and then you'll mindfully shift your posture.

However, if you encounter pain in the meditation that's not connected with a preexisting condition, and your concentration is a little more developed, you should use the pain as an opportunity to develop both your concentration and your discernment. There are three steps in doing this.

*1. Don't change your posture and don't focus attention directly on the pain.* Keep your attention focused on a part of the body you can make comfortable by the way you breathe. Ignore the emergency bulletins that some of the committee members of the mind are sending to you about the pain: that it's going to damage you, that you can't stand it, whatever. Just tell yourself that pain is normal, that the pain before you die may well be worse than this, so it's good to learn how to deal with pain while you're still alive and relatively healthy.

Also remind yourself that the pain is not *your* pain unless you lay claim to it, so why lay claim to it? Just let it be there in its part of the body, while you train yourself to stay firmly in another part of the body. It's like eating an apple with a rotten spot. Eat just the good part of the apple and let the rotten spot go.

2. When the spot where your attention is focused feels really comfortable, **allow comfortable breath sensations to flow from the spot of your focus through the pain,** loosening up any feelings of tension or tightness that may have developed around the pain. (The mind sometimes has an unconscious habit of trying to contain the pain with a shell of tension so that it won't spread, but that just aggravates the pain. Consciously breathing through that shell can disperse it.) Doing this may make the pain go away, or it may not. If it does, you've learned that the way you were breathing was aggravating the pain. Take that as a lesson for the future. If the pain doesn't go away, remind yourself that the duty with regard to pain is not to make it go away. Your duty is to comprehend it. To that aim, if you feel ready to investigate it further, go to step three. If you don't feel ready, you can either stay here with step two or return to step one.

You may find that pains in particular parts of your body respond best to good breath energy spread from other particular spots. For example, a pain in your stomach may be alleviated by developing pleasant breath sensations in the area of the back right behind the stomach. A pain in your right side may be alleviated by developing pleasant breath sensations in the corresponding spot on the left. Pains in the legs may be alleviated by focusing on developing pleasant breath sensations in your spine, starting with the back of the neck and going down through the tail bone and pelvis. There's a lot to explore in this area, and it's something that each person has to learn for him or herself, as we each have idiosyncratic ways of relating to the breath currents and the pains in the body.

3. If the pain persists, and your concentration feels solid enough to deal directly with it, *focus on the sensation of the pain and ask yourself questions about it.*

• For example, is the pain aimed at you, or is it just happening?

• Are you trying to push it away, or are you content just to watch it so that you can understand it?

• Is the pain a single, solid sensation, or is it composed of a series of rapid sensations, arising and passing away in quick succession?

• How do you visualize the pain to yourself? What happens when you change that visual image?

• What happens when you stop labeling it as "pain," and simply call it "sensation"?

• On which side of the pain do you feel you're located? For instance, if the pain is in the leg, do you feel that you're located above the pain? What happens if you tell yourself that you're below the pain?

• Is the pain really where you think it is? For instance, if you feel a pain in your stomach, what happens when you tell yourself that it's actually in your back?

• Is the pain the same thing as the body, or is it something else? (This question works best when you've learned to analyze the way you experience the body from within in terms of four properties: energy, solidity, warmth, and coolness—see the discussion under the fourth jhana, in Part Four. When you look carefully at the sensations of pain, you'll see that they don't correspond to any of these properties. The tendency to conflate the pain with the solid property is what makes the pain seem so persistent.)

• Are you in the line of fire, receiving the pain, or are you simply watching it go past you and disappearing? (A useful perception to hold with regard to pain is that you're riding in the backseat of an old station wagon, the type where the back-seat faces back, and you're simply watching the individual sensations of pain go past you and disappear.)

There are many other questions you might ask yourself about the pain. The important thing is learning to question how you perceive your relationship to the pain. On the one hand, if you keep questioning the pain, you don't let yourself fall into the perception of being its passive victim. You're taking a more active role, as the doer, not letting things take their old, accustomed course. This in itself gives you a measure of independence from the pain. On the other hand, you'll learn that if you apply unskillful perceptions to the pain, they create a bridge into the mind so that the mind feels mental pain—impatience, irritation, worry—over the physical pain. But if you can learn to drop those perceptions, either by replacing them with more skillful perceptions, or by dropping—as soon as you sense them—*all* perceptions that develop around the pain, the bridge is cut. The mind can be perfectly fine, even when the body is in pain. This is an important stage in developing insight.

If you find that the approach of examining the pain in step three isn't giving you any clarity around the pain, and your ability not to feel victimized by the pain is beginning to falter, it's a sign that your concentration is not yet strong enough to deal directly with the pain. Go back to steps one and two.

## WANDERING THOUGHTS

One of the mind's most basic habits is to create thought-worlds and then to inhabit them. This is what the Buddha meant by *becoming*. The ability to engage in becoming is often a useful skill, as it enables you to use your imagination in planning for the future and contemplating lessons from the past. But this skill can become a destructive habit, as you create thought-worlds that develop greed, aversion, delusion, and other destructive mental habits. Your ability to plan for the future can turn into worries that can destroy your peace of mind. Your ability to relive the past can make you miserable in the present.

One of the important skills in meditation is learning how to turn these thought-worlds off and on at will, so that you can think when you need to think, and stop thinking when you don't. In this way, the mind's ability to create thought-worlds won't cause it harm.

In the beginning stages of meditation, you need a few quick and easy rules to help you decide whether a thought is worth following or not. Otherwise, you'll get sucked into every thought-world that can deceive you into thinking that it deserves your attention. So while you're learning to focus on the breath, hold to a simple rule: *Any thought connected with improving your focus on the breath is okay. Any other thought has to be dropped.*

If a thought concerning your work or other responsibilities comes to mind while you're meditating, tell yourself that you'll deal with it right after you leave meditation. Or you may decide to set aside a five or ten minute period at the end of meditation specifically to think about issues in your life that require serious consideration.

If, before you start meditating, you realize that you're facing an important decision in life that might interfere with your meditation, tell yourself that you'll use the meditation period to clear your mind before contemplating the decision. Before meditating, pose whatever questions you want to have answers for, and then drop them. Refuse to pay them any attention if they pop up during the meditation. Focus your attention exclusively on the breath. When you emerge from the meditation, see if an answer presents itself to your awareness. There's no guarantee that the answer will be correct, but at least it's coming from a quiet spot in the mind, and it gives you something to put to the test. If no answer presents itself, your mind is at any rate clearer and sharper than it was before the meditation, putting you in a better position to contemplate the issues you face. But be sure that while you're meditating you don't have anything to do with thoughts about those issues at all.

There are five basic strategies in dealing with wandering thoughts. Each of them helps to strengthen your concentration. But each can also give lessons in discernment.

*1. Return to the breath.*

As soon as you realize that you've lost your focus on the breath, go right back to the breath. Be prepared for the fact that this will happen countless times in the course of your meditation, so be on the lookout for the early warning signs that the mind is about to leave the breath and go somewhere else. Sometimes the mind is like an inchworm at the edge of a leaf. One end is standing on the leaf; the other end is waving around, hoping that another leaf will come its way. As soon as it touches the new leaf, it grabs on and lets go of the old leaf. In other words, part of your mind may be with the breath, but another part is looking for somewhere else to go. The more quickly you can catch sight of the mind at this stage in the process, the better. Simply remind yourself that you're getting bored with the breath because you aren't paying it careful attention. Give yourself a couple of really refreshing breaths, and the front end of the inchworm will get back on the original leaf. As you develop this skill, you begin to see the stages by which the mind creates thought-worlds, which means that you're less likely to be fooled by them.

It's like watching a play from behind the scenes. Ordinarily, when the set crew changes scenes in a play, they drop a curtain before changing the scenery. Only when the new scenery is in place do they raise the curtain, so as not to spoil the illusion that the action has actually moved to another location. The audience, of course, is happy to play along with the illusion. But if you're behind the scenes, you sense the artificiality of it all and you're less taken in.

In the same way, as you focus on the process of thought-creation, rather than on the content of the thoughts, you gain some important insights into how the mind creates thought-worlds for itself—important, because these thought-worlds are a central feature of the unnecessary suffering and stress you're trying to understand and counteract. By focusing not on their content, but on the process by which they're created, you begin to free yourself from their spell.

*2. Focus on the drawbacks of letting yourself stay distracted.*

If simply returning to the breath isn't enough to keep you from continually returning to a series of thoughts, you have to look at the drawbacks of those thoughts. This involves two steps.

a. Ask yourself: If you were to follow those thoughts for the next hour or two, where would they take you? Toward a skillful life or an unskillful one? If they're relatively skillful, are they more skillful than a mind well trained in meditation? No. So while you're meditating they're a waste of time. And what about their entertainment value? If they were a movie, would you pay to see them? Do you really gain anything by following them? What exactly attracts you to those thoughts? Is the pay-off worth the trouble they can cause? Try to find the question that helps you see the thoughts as clearly unworthy of your attention. When you've seen both the allure and the drawbacks of a particular way of thinking, you're learning to see your thoughts as part of a causal process. This helps you to free yourself from their power.

b. Once you're clear on the drawbacks of a particular thought, you can think of a topic that counteracts the emotion or urge lying behind it. For instance, if a thought is motivated by anger, try countering the anger with thoughts of goodwill—first for yourself, then for the person you're angry at. If a thought is motivated by lust, think about the unattractive aspects of the human body—again, starting first with the contents of your own body, then going to the body you're attracted to. A few of these alternative topics are discussed in the section on Disruptive Emotions, below.

Once the new topic has weakened your desire to return to the wandering thought, you can then turn your attention back to the breath.

*3. Ignore the thoughts.*

If the thoughts still keep chattering away, make up your mind that you'll stay with the breath and simply let the thoughts chatter away in another part of your mind. They're like stray dogs: If you give them any attention, they'll keep pestering you. They're like crazy people: Even if you try to chase them away, they'll know that they've gotten to you, and that makes them try to pull you further into their crazy worlds. So you just ignore them. Remind yourself that even though there may be thoughts in the mind, they're just other members of the committee. They haven't destroyed the breath. The breath is still there to focus on. Eventually, from lack of attention, the distracting thoughts will go away on their own.

At the same time, you've learned a lesson in how the act of attention can strengthen or weaken the different potentials in your experience.

*4. Relax the tension that keeps the thought going.*

As you get more sensitive to the subtle breath energies in the body, you'll come to notice that the act of holding onto a thought requires that you develop a slight pattern of tension somewhere in the body, as a kind of marker. Try to locate that pattern of tension, dissolve it with a breath, and the thought will go away from lack of support.

As your concentration gets better, you'll be able to sense these patterns of tension forming even before they become conscious thoughts. You'll come to see the stages by which thought-worlds form. They start as little knots of tension, and then a perception is applied to them, deciding whether to view the knots as physical or as mental phenomena. If the decision is to regard them as mental, then a further perception is applied: What is this thought about?

When you can see these steps, the mind in concentration becomes like a spider on a web: You stay at your spot, and then the sensitivity of the breath-web tells you that a knot of tension is forming at a particular section of the web. You go there, zap the knot with a shot of good breath energy that dissolves it, and then return to your spot.

This strategy gives important lessons in observing how physical and mental phenomena are related to each other.

*5. Suppress the thought.*

If your concentration and discernment aren't yet good enough for these techniques to work with every distracting thought, then when they've all failed with a particularly persistent thought, place the tip of your tongue at the roof of your mouth, clench your teeth, and repeat to yourself over and over that you won't think that thought. Or you might repeat a meditation word, like *buddho,* very quickly in the mind to jam the circuits until the temptation to follow the thought has subsided.

This fifth approach is like a sledgehammer compared to the other approaches, which are more like scalpels. But just as every handyman needs a sledgehammer in his toolkit, every meditator needs a few heavy tools to be prepared for all eventualities. That way unskillful thoughts won't be able to bully you around.

This last approach involves less discernment than the other four, but it does teach a valuable lesson: that you shouldn't overlook a useful strategy just because it seems elementary or crude. Be willing to use whatever works.

Particular types of wandering thoughts—such as lust and anger—have their own counteracting strategies. If you don't have the energy to apply any of these strategies to wandering thoughts, it's a sign that the problem is not restlessness. It's drowsiness.

## DROWSINESS

If you're feeling sleepy, the first step is not to immediately regard it as a sign that you need to rest. Often the mind uses drowsiness as a way to avoid an issue that's about to surface from your inner depths. As a meditator, you want to know about these deeper issues, so you can't let yourself be fooled by this sham drowsiness. You have to test it whenever you encounter it.

*The first test is to change your meditation topic.* When you're with the breath, this can mean changing the rhythm and texture of the breath, or the spot of your focus. For example:

• If short, gentle breathing is making you drowsy, you can try breathing long in and short out, or breathing more heavily.

• If staying with a single focal point is making you drowsy, try focusing on two points at once.

• Or you can move your focal point with every three or five breaths. Follow the roadmap given under step three in the section on Focusing on the Breath, or any other roadmap you may devise.

• Or try evaluating the breath energy in areas you tend to overlook.

Alternatively, you can change your meditation topic to one of the subsidiary topics listed in the Appendix. Contemplation of death—that death could happen at any time—is especially useful when drowsiness is coupled with laziness.

Or you can recite to yourself any poem or chanting passage that you may have memorized.

*The second test is to change your posture.* Get up from your meditation and rub your limbs with your hands. If it's night and you can see the night sky, look up at the stars to freshen the mind. Wash your face. Then return to the sitting position.

*The third test is to get up and do walking meditation.* If that doesn't remove the drowsiness, try walking carefully backwards to see if the fear of running into anything will keep you awake.

If the drowsiness remains, it's a sign that the body needs to rest. Lie down and meditate until you fall asleep, first promising yourself that you'll get up and meditate again as soon as you wake up. You won't keep wallowing in the pleasure of lying down.

### DELUSION CONCENTRATION

Closely related to drowsiness is a state of mind called delusion concentration. The mind is still, but you're not clearly aware of where your attention is focused. When you come out of it, you may wonder whether you were asleep or awake. This can happen when the breath gets comfortable but you don't spread your awareness to other parts of the body. You're focused on a small area, and when the breath in that area gets very refined and comfortable, you lose track of it and slip into a pleasant, still, but blurry state of mind.

One way to prevent this is, as soon as the breath gets comfortable, to immediately start surveying the rest of the body. Try to notice how the breath energy is flowing in all the nooks and crannies of the body, even down to the spaces between the fingers and toes. Alternatively, you can visualize the various parts of the body—the bones, the organs—and see if the breath energy is spreading smoothly to those parts.

The important principle here is that when the mind is comfortable, it needs some work to do. Otherwise, it will drift off into drowsiness. As long as the work stays within the confines of the body, it won't disturb your concentration. In fact, it will make the concentration even stronger and more resilient.

The phenomenon of falling into an "air pocket"—i.e., sitting very still and then suddenly being awakened by your head falling forward—comes from the same causes and can be cured in the same ways.

## EXTERNAL NOISES

If you find yourself complaining about external noises while you're meditating, remind yourself that the noise isn't bothering you. You're bothering the noise. Can you let the noise exist without your commenting on it? After all, the noise has no intention to bother you.

Also, think of your body as a screen on a large window. The noise is like the wind going through the screen. In other words, you offer no resistance to the noise, but you don't let yourself be affected by it. It goes right through you without making physical or mental contact.

## TROUBLES WITH THE BREATH ITSELF

1. Probably one of the most discouraging obstacles to breath meditation is *an inability to feel the in-and-out breath.* This often comes from an earlier physical or emotional experience that has caused you to block off your sensation of the body. You may require time to build up a sensitivity to the felt reality of the breath in the body, or to feel at ease with that sensitivity. This is an area that requires patience.

There are two possible approaches.

• One is to ask yourself where you *do* feel the breath. It may be only in the head or at some other isolated part of the body. Still, that gives you something to start with. Focus on that area gently but steadily, with an attitude of goodwill for it, telling yourself that you belong there. When you find that you can stay there with a sense of ease, gradually try to expand your sense of awareness right around that spot. What part of the body is right next to it? In which direction do you feel that part? (Your inner sense of the parts of your body may not be in alignment with how the body looks from the outside, but don't let that concern you right now. Where do you *feel* the next part?) If a sense of fear arises, go back to the original area. Wait for a day or so, and then try expanding your awareness slightly again. Keep this up, back and forth, until you can inhabit the enlarged area with a sense of confidence. Be patient. If any specific fears or memories come up as you try to expand your awareness in this way, talk them over with someone whose judgment you trust.

• A second approach is to drop the breath for the time being and to develop the brahmaviharas (see Part One, section I, above) as your basic meditation exercise until you feel confident enough to try working with the breath again.

2. Another problem that can often be discouraging is *an inability to find a comfortable breath*. No matter how you adjust the breath, it doesn't feel right. There are several ways to approach this problem.

• Ask yourself if you're being too demanding. Does the breath feel okay? Are you trying to force it to be better than okay? If that's what's happening, be patient. Stick with the okay breath and give it some time. Your impatience may be putting too much strain on it. Allow it some time to relax and develop on its own.

• Ask yourself if you're pinching the end of the out-breath to clearly mark it off from the following in-breath, or vice versa.

This limits the ability of the breath to flow smoothly. If this is the case, allow the end of each out-breath to meld smoothly with the beginning of the following in-breath, and vice versa, so that the still moment between the breaths can have a chance to let a sense of ease spread through the body.

• Remind yourself that each breath will have at least one part—at the beginning, in the middle, or near the end—that feels more comfortable than not breathing. Look for that part of the breath and allow yourself to appreciate it. When this calms you down, the other parts of the breath cycle will be able to relax.

• Ask yourself if you're focusing too hard in one spot. There's a common tendency, when you're focused on a particular part of the body, to put pressure on it—usually blocking or straining the way the blood flows in that part of the body. See if you can release that pressure but still maintain focus on that spot.

• Ask yourself if the way you visualize the breath to yourself is part of the problem. For example, do you visualize it as coming into the body only through one tiny spot, such as the nose? If so, that might be restricting the breath. Try visualizing the body as a sponge, with breath coming in and out easily through all the pores. Or you can ask yourself if you visualize the breath as unwilling to come into the body. If so, you'll find yourself having to force it in. Try visualizing it as *wanting* to come into the body, and all you have to do is allow it in.

• Ask yourself if you're unconsciously forcing the breath to comply with any cartoon ideas you might have of what comfortable breathing should feel like. People often assume that slow, long breathing is more comfortable than short, fast breathing, but that's not always the case. Remind yourself that what counts as comfortable breathing is determined by what the body needs right now, so try to be more sensitive to those needs.

• Ask yourself if you're trying to control the breath too much. You can test this by focusing attention on a part of the body where you have no sense of being able to control the movement of the breath, such as the base of the spine.

• If none of these approaches work, switch the topic of your focus to a theme that you find pleasurable and inspiring, such as goodwill, generosity (thinking of the times you were generous of your own free will), gratitude (thinking of people who went out of their way to help you), or virtue (thinking of cases where you or someone you admire behaved in ways you find noble and inspiring). Allow yourself to think about that theme for a while without paying attention to the breath. When the mind feels refreshed, try to notice how you're breathing while you're with that theme. The breath will have found a comfortable rhythm on its own. That will give you some ideas about how to breathe comfortably.

3. A third common problem is *an inability to feel breath sensations in different parts of the body.* This is often a problem of perception: The breath sensations are there, but you don't recognize them as such. Part of your mind may think that it's impossible for there to be breath energies flowing through the body. If that's the case, treat this as an exercise in imagination: Allow yourself to imagine that breathing energy can flow through the nerves, and imagine it flowing in some of the patterns recommended in the basic instructions. Or imagine it flowing in the opposite directions. At some point, you will actually start to feel the movement of energy in one part of the body or another, and then this will no longer be an exercise in imagination.

In the meantime, survey the body and relax any patterns of tension you may feel in its various parts. Start with the hands and work up the arms. Then start with the feet and work up through the legs, the back, the neck, and into the head. Then do the front of the torso. The more relaxed the body, the more easily the breath energy will flow, and the more likely that you'll be able to sense the flow.

## UNUSUAL ENERGIES & SENSATIONS

**Pressure.** As you release tension or tightness in different parts of the body, it can often give rise to unusually strong or unbalanced energies or sensations. This is normal, and these energies, if left alone, can often work themselves out. However, there are two cases where they can become a problem.

1. The first is when the release is not complete—when energy released from one area gets stuck in another, creating a strong sense of pressure. Two common areas where pressure tends to build up are in the head and around the heart. If the pressure is in the head, check to see whether the energy needs to drain down the front of the throat or down the spine. First focus on opening the energy channel down the front of your throat, and place your attention in the middle of the chest. Think of the energy draining down the channel in the throat to the area where you're focused, both during the in-breath and during the out.

If that doesn't work, consciously trace the energy channels down either side of the spine to see if there's a point of blockage at any point. If you find one, think of it relaxing. Do this all the way down the spine. Focus your attention at your tailbone. Then visualize the breath going down the spine—again, both during the in-breath and during the out—and then flowing through your tailbone into the air.

If the pressure is in the middle of the chest, visualize opening the energy channels going out your arms through the palms of your hands. Focus your attention at the palms of your hands and think of breath energy radiating out from your chest—both during the in-breath and during the out—and going out through your palms.

You can also try a similar visualization with energy channels going down your legs and out through the soles of your feet.

As you open these channels, don't think of pushing the energy into them. In particular, don't think that you're trying to push air into them. The breath you're working with is energy, not air. And energy flows best when it's not pressured. Simply think, "Allow." And be patient. Try to distinguish between the flow of the blood—which, because it's liquid, can build up pressure when it runs up against something solid—and the flow of the breath, which as an energy doesn't need to build up pressure, as it can flow right through solids.

If you feel excess pressure in other parts of the body, try connecting those parts, in your imagination, with the energy channels going out the arms or legs.

2. The other main cause of excess pressure in different parts of the body is when, in an effort to speed up the movement of the breath energy in the body, you push it too much. Here again, the key word is "allow." Allow the energy to flow. Don't push it. A comfortable energy, when pushed, becomes uncomfortable. Be patient. Visualize a subtle breath energy that, as soon as you're aware that you've started breathing in, has already spread throughout the body. After a while, you'll sense that it really is there.

**A tightness that doesn't respond to the breath.** If there are islands of tightness in the body that won't dissolve no matter how comfortable the breath, you have to work around them. The more directly you focus on them, the worse they may get. So breathe gently around their edges and give them some space. They often represent members of your inner committee who don't trust your good intentions, so you simply have to let them be. Be patient with them. At some point they'll dissolve on their own.

**Bands of tension running through the body.** Check first to see if the bands of tension really are bands, or if the mind is playing connect-the-dots with them. In other words, there are occasions when the mind notices spots of tension in different parts of the body and connects them under a single perception of tension. This creates the sensation that the isolated spots are part of a single sensation.

To test if this is the case, imagine that your awareness is a set of buzz-saw blades, quickly and repeatedly cutting the bands of tension into isolated pieces wherever it notices them. If this lightens the sense of tension, then hold that perception in mind. The problem is not with the tension as much as it was with the perception that labeled the spots of tension as bands. Keep refusing to believe in that band-perception, replacing it with the perception of saw blades as long as necessary.

If the bands of tension are in the head and seem to surround the head, an alternative way of shifting the perception is to hold in mind the image that your head is larger than the bands of tension, and that the larger part of the head is filled with soft energy that allows the bands to dissipate.

If the sense of a band of tension remains in spite of the new perceptions, then it's a sign the band corresponds to an area of the body that's starved of breath energy. As you breathe in, think of the breath energy going immediately to that part of the body. Allow the in-breath to be as long as it needs to be to give that area a sense of being nourished.

If, after several minutes of trying this approach, the bands of tension don't respond, then ignore them for a while. Try these various approaches again later when your concentration has improved.

**A lack of sensation.** As you survey the various parts of your body, you may find that there are some parts where you feel no sensation at all: your shoulder, for example, or part of your back. It seems as if that part of the body is missing. When this is the case, try to be conscious of the parts that you *can* sense on either side of the missing part. For example, with the shoulder: Try to be aware of your neck and your upper arm. Then try to see where the energy in those two parts connects. You may be surprised to see that there is a connection, but it's not where your shoulder "should" be—and because it's not where it should be, you've unconsciously been blocking it. Allow it to open up and over time your sense of those parts of the body will adjust and the missing part of the body will get more nourishment from the breath. It'll reappear in your awareness.

**A sense of fullness.** This sensation often comes when the breath energy dissolves some of its inner blockages, and areas that were starved of energy suddenly fill up. This relates to one of the factors of jhana: rapture. In strong cases, it can feel as if you're drowning in the fullness. Some people find this pleasant, but others find it threatening. If you've ever come close to drowning, this can easily bring up a sense of fear. The way to counteract the fear is to remind yourself that you're surrounded by air, and the body can breathe as much as it likes. Relax your hands and feet, and keep them relaxed. Then see if you can find the aspect of the fullness that's pleasant. Focus on that. Or simply maintain your focus on your usual point of focus in the body, and remind yourself that the fullness, if left alone, will eventually dissipate into a sense of stillness and ease.

Another group of people who find this sense of fullness threatening are those who fear that they're losing control. The solution again is not to focus on the fullness, but to stay focused on your usual point of focus, and remember that the fullness will pass.

**A feeling of density.** Sometimes, as the mind settles down, the body feels so solid and dense that breathing becomes a chore. One possible reason for this is that you're subconsciously holding onto the perception of the body as a solid object, and of the breath as something that has to be pushed through the solidity. The solution is consciously to change your perception. For instance, you can remind yourself that the breath is actually your primary sensation of the body: The energy of the breath is there first, and the sense of solidity comes later. So you don't have to push the breath through a wall of solidity. Let it flow freely wherever it wants. Another useful perception is to think of all the space around the body and in-between the atoms in the body. Even within the atoms, there's more space than matter. Everything is permeated by space. As you hold this perception in mind, the difficulty in breathing will go away.

Another possible reason for the sense that the body is too solid to breathe is that the mind may be so quiet that you don't *need* to breathe (see the discussion under The Fourth Jhana in Part Four.) You keep on trying to push the breath through the body more out of habit than of need. So tell yourself, "If the body needs to breathe, it'll breathe on its own. You don't have to force it to breathe."

**Dizziness.** If this problem is caused by the meditation, it can come from an imbalance in your focus or an imbalance in the breath.

An imbalance in your focus can come from focusing too heavily in the head. Move your focus lower in the body, lighten up a bit so that you're not restricting the flow of blood in the area where you're focused, and stay away from the head for a while.

An imbalance in the breath might come from hyperventilating: breathing heavily too fast. It can also come from suppressing the breath or spending too much time with refined breathing. Try breathing in a way that avoids these extremes. If this doesn't take care of the dizziness, it wasn't caused by the meditation. It may be a sign of physical illness.

## JUDGING YOUR PROGRESS

As I noted in the Introduction, the basic strategy of training the mind to put an end to suffering is to reflect on your actions and to question how skillful they are, so that you can keep refining your skill. Because meditation is an action, the same strategy applies here. To develop it as a skill, you have to learn how to evaluate how you're doing—what's working, what's not working—so that your skill can grow. In fact, evaluation is such an important part of meditation that it's a factor of jhana, which we will discuss in Part Four. This sort of evaluation is what turns into the discernment that ultimately leads to release.

So remember: There is such a thing as a good session and a not-so-good session of meditation. You want to learn how to judge the difference. However, the ability to judge your actions is, itself, a skill that takes some time to master. If you've ever worked toward mastering a physical skill or craft—such as woodworking, cooking, or playing a sport or musical instrument—think of how you developed your powers of judgment so that they actually helped you gain mastery. Then apply the same principles to the meditation. A few useful principles to keep in mind are these:

*Useful judgments focus on actions, not on your worth as a person or a meditator.*

If you find yourself getting depressed about yourself for not being able to do things right, or conceited when they *do* go right, remind yourself that that kind of judgment is a waste of time. Negative self-judgments sap your ability to stick with the meditation; positive self-judgments—even though they may encourage you in the short run—will ultimately get in the way of your progress, blinding you to your mistakes or setting up false expectations. If you find yourself in the downward spiral of negatively judging yourself for judging yourself, remember the image of the inner committee. Find a member who can gently but firmly remind the self-judging voice that it's wasting your time. The more good-natured humor you can bring to the situation, the better. Then focus on your next breath, and then the next.

The one area where it *is* useful to evaluate yourself is in reading your tendency to be overly positive or overly negative about your abilities. If you know that you have a tendency in either of those directions, use that knowledge to temper your judgments.

A friendly, "Oops. There it goes again," can often help bring you to your senses.

*Regard your meditation as a work in progress.* You're not here to pass final judgment on yourself or your actions. You're judging your actions so that you can perform them more skillfully the next time around. As you make a judgment, think of yourself not as a judge on a courtroom bench, passing a verdict on an accused person, but as a craftsperson on a workbench, judging how your work is going, and making changes when you see you've made a mistake.

*Mistakes are normal.* It's through mistakes that you learn. The people who understand meditation best aren't the ones for whom everything goes smoothly. They're the ones who make mistakes and then figure out how not to make them again. So view each mistake as an opportunity to figure things out. Don't let it get you down. In fact, if you're going to take pride in anything, take pride in your willingness to notice and learn from mistakes.

*The relation between actions and results is complex, so don't jump to quick conclusions about what caused what in your meditation.* Sometimes the results you get right now are coming from things you're doing right now; sometimes they're coming from things you did yesterday, or last week, or even further in the past. This is why an approach that worked yesterday might not work today. Learn how to reserve judgment until you've had time to watch your meditation again and again over time.

And don't keep harping on about how much better your meditation was in the past than it is today. The extent to which it *was* good wasn't caused by thinking about meditations further in the past. It was caused by looking at the breath in the present. So learn from that lesson and look at the breath in the present *now*. Also, the past meditation may not have been as good as you thought. The fact that things aren't yet going well today is caused by the fact that you still have more to learn. So to learn some of that "more," watch the breath and your mind more carefully right now.

*Don't be surprised by sudden reversals in your meditation.*

These, too, are caused by the complexity of how actions give their results. When things are going so well that the mind grows still without any effort on your part, don't get careless or overly confident. Keep up your alertness. When your mood is so bad that you can't stay with even the first step in the meditation instructions, don't give up. View it as an opportunity to learn more about how the principle of causality works in the mind. Something must have caused the sudden change, so look for it. At the same time, this is a good opportunity to call to mind your sense of the inner observer, to be patient in stepping back and observing bad moods. This way, whether the sudden reversal is for the better or the worse, you learn a valuable lesson: how to keep your inner observer separate from whatever else is going on so that you can watch things more carefully.

*Don't compare yourself with others.*

Your mind is your mind; their mind is theirs. It's like being in a hospital and comparing yourself to other patients in the ward. You don't gain anything from gloating over the fact that you're recovering from your illness faster than they are from theirs. You don't gain anything from making yourself miserable because they're recovering faster than you. You have to focus total attention on your own recovery.

*While meditating, don't compare your practice to what you've read in books, this one included.*

The books are there for you to read when you're not meditating. While you're meditating, you want to focus on the breath.

The books simply give you ideas about what *might* happen. You learn even more from watching what *is* happening and—if it's called for—figuring out on the spot how to make what's happening go better.

## MAINTAINING MOTIVATION

Training the mind is a long-term project. It requires a degree of maturity to keep motivated when the novelty and initial enthusiasm have worn off. Especially when progress is slow, you may find yourself overcome with boredom, discouragement, impatience, or doubt. If your motivation is flagging because of any of these emotions, see the recommendations given for dealing with them in the following section.

However, there are times when your motivation flags simply because the demands of your personal life or work become so pressing that they squeeze away whatever time or energy you need to meditate. If this is happening, you have to keep reminding yourself of the importance of meditating: that if your mind isn't trained, it can easily respond to the demands of your daily life in unskillful ways.

The first point to remember is that "pressing" doesn't always mean "important." Learn how to distinguish which external demands can be put aside for a while so that you can get your mind together.

The second point to remember is that the world won't provide you with time to meditate. You have to make the time yourself.

Third, remember that the time you take to meditate isn't taken away from the people you love or are responsible for. It's actually a gift to them in terms of your improved state of mind.

Fourth, remember that the improved state of your mind will also help simplify your life and make it more manageable.

So to make sure that you keep making time on a continuing basis, try adding a few new voices to your inner committee, or strengthening them if they're already there—the voices that will give you pep talks and motivate you to stay on course. Which ones will be most effective for you, you have to observe for yourself. These will vary from person to person, and even in the same person will vary from time to time.

Here are a few voices that other meditators have found effective:

• *The voice of heedfulness:* the one that reminds you of the unnecessary stress and suffering an untrained mind can cause for itself and for those around you. This is the voice that also tells you, "If you don't train your mind, who's going to train it for you? And if you don't do it now, don't think that it'll get easier as you get older."

• *The voice of compassion* reminds you of the ways in which meditating is an active expression of goodwill to yourself and to those around you. You started meditating because you wanted something better than the life you had. If you really loved yourself—and your loved ones—would you let that opportunity slide? This voice is strengthened when you gain a sense of how to breathe comfortably, for then you can remind yourself, especially when you feel frazzled, of just how good it feels to spend some time with nourishing breath.

• *The voice of healthy pride* reminds you of the satisfaction that comes from doing something well. This is the voice that reminds you of how good you feel when you've managed to behave skillfully in areas where you weren't so skillful before. Don't you want to expand your range of skills even further?

• *The voice of a healthy sense of shame* grows out of healthy pride. It reminds you of some of the ways in which you've let the unskillful members of your inner committee take over even when you knew better. Do you want to keep being their slave? And if there really are people in the world who can read minds, what would they think if they read yours? (This sense of shame is healthy in that it's directed not at you as a person, but at your actions.)

• *The voice of inspiration* reminds you of the examples set by other meditators in the past. They did something noble with their lives; don't you want to live a noble life, too? This voice is strengthened when you read about others who have overcome difficulties in their meditation and not only achieved true peace of mind but also left behind a good example for the world. Your sense of inspiration can also be strengthened by associating with other meditators and gaining energy from the group.

• *The voice of a wise inner parent* promises you a little reward to get you through difficult patches in the practice: a harmless sensory pleasure you'll grant yourself if you stick to your meditation schedule.

• *The voice of good-natured humor* points out how foolish some of your rationalizations for not practicing would look if you stepped back from them a bit. Not that you're more foolish than the norm—just that the human norm is pretty foolish. Good-natured humor about yourself comes from the ability to step back from your actions, just as discernment does. That's why famous meditation masters have such sharp senses of humor. Your foibles and rationalizations, when you can laugh at them, lose a lot of their power.

So try to gain a feel for which of these voices would stir your mind to action, and give yourself pep talks tailored to your own psychology.

At the same time, listen to recorded Dhamma talks and find things to read that will remind you of the values of the practice. This will help to keep you on course.

If your time really is at a premium, remember that you don't have to sit with your eyes closed when training the mind. As many teachers have said, if you have time to breathe, you have time to meditate even while engaged in other activities.

Also, you might find it helpful to remind yourself that if you're really busy, you're not too busy to meditate. You're too busy *not* to meditate. You owe it to yourself and to those around you to keep your batteries well charged.

## DISRUPTIVE EMOTIONS

When dealing with disruptive emotions, it's useful to remember the three types of fabrication mentioned in the Introduction: bodily fabrication (the in-and-out breath); verbal fabrication (directed thought and evaluation); and mental fabrication (feelings and perceptions). These are the building blocks from which emotions are fashioned. To get yourself out of an unskillful emotion, you change the building blocks. Don't allow yourself to be fooled into thinking that the emotion is telling you what you *really* feel. Every emotion is a bundle of fabrications, so a skillful emotion you consciously fabricate is no less really "you" than an unskillful emotion you've fabricated unconsciously out of force of habit.

So learn how to experiment with adjusting the various types of fabrication. Sometimes just changing the way you breathe will pull you out of an unskillful emotion; at other times you have to fiddle with the other forms of fabrication to see what works for you.

Here again the image of the committee is a useful background perception: Whatever the emotion, it's simply one of the committee members—or a disruptive faction—claiming to speak for the whole committee and trying to overthrow the members who want to meditate.

The number one lesson in dealing with disruptive emotions is that you have to identify with the members who want to benefit from the meditation. If you don't, none of these methods will work for long. If you do, the battle is half-won.

You will have to explore and experiment on your own to see which strategies of refabrication work for your particular emotions, but here are a few possibilities to help you get started:

**Boredom.** This usually comes from not paying careful attention to what you're doing. If you feel that nothing is happening in the meditation, remind yourself that you're right at the ideal spot to observe your mind. If you're not seeing anything, you're not looking. So try to look more carefully at the breath, or make an effort to see potential distractions more quickly. Remember that the boredom itself is a distraction. It comes, and then it goes. In other words, it's not the case that nothing is happening. Boredom is happening. The fact that you're identifying with it means that you missed the steps in its formation. Look more carefully the next time.

A useful perception to hold in mind is that you're like a wildlife observer. You can't make a date with the wildlife to come by a particular place at a particular time. You have to go to a place where the wildlife tends to pass by—such as a watering hole—and then sit there: very alert, so that you can hear them coming, but also very still, so that you don't scare them away. The breath in the present moment is the mind's watering hole—where the movements of the mind most clearly show themselves—so you're at the right spot. Now all you have to do is learn how to master the skill of staying both still and alert.

**Discouragement.** This comes from comparing yourself unfavorably with your ideas about how you should be progressing. In addition to rereading the section on Judging Your Progress, read some of the stories in the Theragatha and Therigatha in the Pali Canon, which are available at Access to Insight, online. These are verses of monks and nuns who tell of their troubles in meditating before finally gaining awakening. Hold in mind the perception that if they could overcome their problems—which were often severe—you can overcome yours.

Also, don't be embarrassed or afraid to give yourself pep talks as you meditate. A "can-do" attitude is what makes all the difference, so encourage the members of your committee that can provide that. It may feel artificial at first—especially if the "can't-do" members have long been in charge of the discussion—but after a while you'll start seeing results, and positive attitudes won't seem so artificial anymore.

And always remember: A bad session of meditation is always better than no meditation. With a bad session, there's at least hope that you'll come to understand why it's bad. With no meditation, there's no hope at all.

**Worry & anxiety.** These restless emotions feed on the perception that if you worry enough about the future, you're better prepared for whatever dangers it holds. That perception is foolish. Remind yourself that the future is highly uncertain. You don't know what dangers will come your way, but you *do* know that strengthened mindfulness, alertness, and discernment are the best preparation for any unexpected emergencies. The best way to develop those qualities is to get back to the breath. Then try to breathe in as soothing a way as possible to counteract the irritated breathing that was feeding the restlessness.

If you're suffering from a sense of free-floating anxiety—ill-at-ease without knowing why you're feeling ill-at-ease—you may be suffering from a vicious circle, with anxious feelings causing anxious breathing, and anxious breathing feeding anxious feelings. Try breaking the circle by very consciously and consistently breathing in a deep, soothing rhythm that engages all the muscles in your abdomen, all the way down. With the in-breath, breathe as deeply into the abdomen as you can, even to the point where the breath feels a little too full. Then let the breath out in a smooth way. Relax all the muscles in your head and shoulders, so that the abdomen is doing all the work. This rhythm may not feel comfortable at first, but it does cut the circle. After a few minutes, let the breath return to a rhythm that feels more easeful. Keep this up as long as you can, and the feelings of anxiety should grow weaker.

This deep abdominal breathing can also help relieve stress-induced headaches.

**Feelings of grief.** If sorrow over the loss of a loved one—or of what was a loving relationship—invades your meditation, the proper way to deal with your grief depends on whether you've had the opportunity elsewhere in your life to give enough expression to it. The sense of "enough" here will vary from case to case, but if you genuinely feel that you need to give more expression to your grief, find an appropriate time and place to do so. Then, when you feel ready to meditate, make a resolve to dedicate the merit of the meditation to the memory of the person you've lost. The conviction that this is actually helpful to the other person—wherever he or she may now be—allows you to benefit from the inner stability that meditation can provide you during times of need.

Healthy grieving is a complex process, for it requires recognizing what was special about the other person and the relationship, but also recognizing what's not: the fact that it ended. Every relationship has to end at some time or another. That's the story of human life. You need to build the inner strength that can allow you to maintain a sense of well-being in spite of the inevitable losses that life throws at everyone. This is one of the reasons why people meditate.

To find this inner strength doesn't mean that you're being disloyal to the other person or to the love you felt for that person. You're showing that you can be a stronger person for having had that relationship. For many people, the difficult part of grief lies in knowing when to focus less on what was special about the relationship and more on what was not special, without feeling disloyal. If you never make the shift, your grief becomes self-indulgent and prevents you from being of use to yourself and those you love. If you have trouble making the shift, talk it over with someone whose judgment you trust.

**Painful memories.** If, while you're meditating, your mind is overwhelmed with the memory of someone who harmed you, remind yourself that one of the best gifts you can give yourself is to forgive that person. This doesn't mean that you have to feel love for that person, simply that you promise yourself not to seek revenge for what that person did. You're better off not trying to settle old scores, for scores in life—as opposed to sports—never come to a final tally. The wisest course is to unburden yourself of the weight of resentment and cut the cycle of retribution that would otherwise keep you ensnarled in an ugly back and forth that could go on for years. Express a brief phrase of goodwill for the person—"May you mend your ways and follow the path to true happiness"—and then return to the breath.

If you have memories of people you've harmed, remember that remorse doesn't undo the harm you did, and it can actually weaken your confidence that you can change your ways. Simply remind yourself that you never want to harm anyone ever again, and then spread goodwill to the person you've harmed—wherever that person may be right now—then to yourself, and then to all living beings.

Thinking of all living beings helps to remind you that you're not the only one who has harmed others in the past. We've all harmed one another many times through innumerable lifetimes. However, this type of thinking also reminds you that the opportunities for harm are many, so you have to make the resolve to treat everyone with care. If you're ever going to get out of the cycle of harm in the world, you have to start with *your* resolve not to engage in harm. You can't wait for the resolve to start in other people first.

Finally, make a promise to yourself that you'll dedicate the merit of your meditation to people you've harmed. Then return to the breath.

The same principle applies if you have memories of times when someone needed your help but you didn't give it. If the memory is of a time when you *couldn't* give help to someone who needed it, reread the discussion of equanimity in Part One, section I.

**Lust.** Lust comes from focusing on the attractive perceptions you build around a person or a relationship, and ignoring the unattractive side. It gets aggravated by the type of breathing that habitually accompanies your fantasies. So your approach has to be two-pronged.

• First, to weaken the voice that insists on some pleasure *right now,* breathe in a way that relaxes any tension wherever you find it in your body. A good place to start is on the back of your hands.

• Second, introduce unattractive perceptions into your fantasies. If you're focusing on the attractiveness of the other person's body, focus on the unattractive parts right under the skin. If you're focusing on an attractive narrative about the relationship, visualize the other person doing or saying something that really repels you. For instance, think about the stupid or demeaning things you've done under the power of lust, and visualize the other person laughing contemptuously about them behind your back. If, however, contempt fires you up, think about something else that you know will turn you off. Think, for instance, of all the strings that come with a sexual relationship, and how much better off you are not getting entangled. Then get back to the breath.

These reflections, by the way, are not just for monks or nuns. Laypeople in a committed relationship need tools to keep their minds from wandering outside of the relationship. And even within the relationship, there are plenty of times when they need to keep lust under control. And if you're not in a committed relationship, you suffer if you can't turn off thoughts of lust at will. Society at large may extol and encourage lust, but uncontrolled lust has done untold damage. That's why you need tools to counteract it, not only while meditating, but also as you go through the day. Only when lust can be kept within bounds do the good qualities that thrive in its absence have a chance to grow.

**Romantic infatuation.** This is a variant of lust in which you're focused less on the other person's body and more on the stories you can manufacture about how you and the other person will find happiness and understanding together. Remind yourself of how your romantic fantasies in the past led to disappointment. Do you expect your current fantasies to be any more reliable? Once you can see the danger of falling for these fantasies, inject an element of reality into them to make them less attractive. Think of the other person doing something that you find really disappointing, such as being unfaithful to you, until the act of fantasizing no longer holds any appeal.

**Anger.** As with lust, you deal with anger first by looking for where it has created centers of tightness in your body. The chest and the stomach are good places to start, as are the hands. Breathe in a way that releases that tightness.

Then try some perceptions that will counteract the anger. Thoughts of goodwill are often recommended as the ideal antidote, but there are times when you're in no mood for thoughts of goodwill. So think about the stupid things you do or say under the power of anger, and visualize the person with whom you're angry feeling satisfied to see you act stupidly. Do you want to give that person that sort of satisfaction? This line of thinking can often calm you down to the point where you can think more clearly.

Then reflect on the fact that if you want everything to go the way you like, you're in the wrong realm. You'd have to be in heaven. But here you're in the human realm. Human history is filled with people doing disagreeable things. So drop the perception that you or your loved ones are being especially victimized. Mistreatment is a common thing, and anger is not going to help you deal with it effectively. You've got to clear your head if you want your response to injustice to have a good effect. So try to develop some equanimity around the fact that injustice is universal, and then see what you can do most effectively in response to this particular instance of it.

Another strategy is to think of whatever goodness has been done by the people you're angry at. It's rare that people have no goodness to them at all. If you refuse to see that goodness, you can't trust yourself to act in skillful ways around those people, and your own heart becomes dry.

A traditional image for this strategy is that you're crossing a desert—hot, tired, and trembling with thirst—and you come across a little water in a cow's footprint. If you were to scoop it up with your hand, you'd muddy the water. So you do what you have to do: Get down on all fours and slurp up the water directly from the footprint. Your posture while doing this may not look very dignified, but this is not a time to worry about how you look. You've got to give top priority to your survival. In the same way, if you feel that it's beneath you to look for the goodness done by someone you're angry at, you deprive yourself of the water you need to keep your own goodness alive. So try looking for that goodness, to see if it makes it easier to develop thoughts of goodwill. And remember: It's for your own sake as much as for theirs.

If you can't think of any goodness done by the people you're angry at, then take pity on them: They're digging themselves into a deep hole.

**Jealousy.** Jealousy is a particular type of anger that comes when other people experience good fortune at what you see is your expense—as when a colleague at work gets praise that you feel you deserve, or when a person you're infatuated with falls in love with someone else. In addition to the anger, jealousy adds perceptions of disappointment and wounded pride. In every case it comes from pinning your hopes for happiness on something under someone else's control.

One way of dealing with jealousy is to remind yourself that you're going to be a slave to it as long as you keep defining your happiness and sense of self-worth by things outside your control. Isn't it time to seriously start looking for happiness inside instead? You can also ask yourself if you want to hoard all the happiness and good fortune in the world for yourself. If so, what kind of person are you? If there have been times in the past when you've enjoyed making other people jealous, remind yourself that the jealousy you're currently experiencing is the inevitable payback. Isn't it time to get out of that vicious cycle?

Perhaps one of the most useful perceptions in dealing with jealousy is to step back and take a larger view of life and the world as a whole, to gain a sense of how petty the things you're jealous about really are. Think of the Buddha's vision of the human world: people floundering like fish in small puddles, fighting over water that is drying up. Is it worth your while to keep fighting over things that are petty and diminishing, or would you rather find a better source of happiness?

After thinking in these ways, take some time to develop the sublime attitude of equanimity and—if you're feeling up for it—throw in a little empathetic joy as well.

**Impatience.** When the practice isn't giving results as fast as you'd desire, remember that the problem isn't with the desire *per se*. You've simply focused it on the wrong place: on the results rather than on the causes that will produce those results. It's like driving a car to a mountain on the horizon. If you spend all your time looking at the mountain, you'll drive off the road. You have to focus your attention on the road and follow it each inch along the way. That will take you to the mountain.

So when you're feeling impatient with the meditation, remember that you have to focus your desire on staying with the breath, on being mindful and alert, and on all the other parts of the practice that count as causes. If you focus your desire on developing the causes well, the results will have to come.

If impatience comes from a desire to get past the meditation so that you can get on with the rest of your life, remember that the rest of your life has left your mind in need of some healing medicine. Meditation is just that medicine, like the cream you'd rub on a rash. You can't just rub the cream on and then wash it off. You have to let it stay there so that it can do its healing work. In the same way, you have to give the breath and all the skillful qualities that you're developing around it time to do their work.

And remember that meditation is not something you "get past." Just as your body will need medicine as long as it's exposed to the ravages of the world, your mind will need the healing medicine of meditation as long as you live.

**Doubt.** This emotion comes in two forms: doubt about yourself, which is covered under Discouragement, above; and doubt about the practice. This latter doubt can be overcome in two ways.

• The first is to read about the example of the Buddha and his noble disciples. They were (and are) people of wisdom and integrity. They taught for free. They had no reason to misrepresent the truth to anyone. It's rare to find teachers like that in the world, so you should give them the benefit of the doubt.

• The second way is to remind yourself that the practice can be truly judged only by a person who is true. Are you true in sticking with the breath? Are you true in observing when your mind is acting in skillful ways and when it's not? Could you be more true in these areas? You'll be able to overcome your doubt only if you're truly observant and give the teachings a truly fair and earnest try, pushing yourself beyond your normal limits. Regardless of whether the practice ultimately will pan out to be true, you can only gain by learning to be more observant and earnest, so the energy you put into developing these qualities is sure not to be a waste.

## VISIONS & OTHER UNCANNY PHENOMENA

When the mind starts to quiet down, unusual intuitions can sometimes appear: visions, voices, and other uncanny phenomena. Sometimes they convey true information; sometimes false. The true information is especially dangerous, because it leads you to trust whatever pops into your mind, so that you start falling for the things that are false. Intuitions of this sort can also lead to strong conceit, as you begin to feel that you're somehow special. This pulls you far off the path.

For this reason, the general rule of thumb with regard to these things is to leave them be. Remember: *Not everything that arises in a still mind is trustworthy.* So don't feel that you're missing out on something important if you don't get involved with these things. Only if you're under the personal supervision of a teacher who is skilled in handling them should you risk getting involved. The best information a book like this can offer is on how to pull yourself out of them. For instance:

**Signs.** Sometimes when the mind settles down, a light may appear to the mind, or you may hear a high-pitched sound in your ears. Or there may be an unusual sensation related to any of your other senses: a smell, a taste, a tactile sensation. If this happens, don't leave the breath. These are simply signs that you're settling down, so regard them as you would signs on the side of a road. When you see a sign that you're entering a city, you don't leave the road to drive on the sign. You stay on the road, and that will get you further into the city.

**Visions.** As the mind begins to settle down—or if it leaves the breath in a lapse of mindfulness—you may see a vision of yourself, another person, or another place in space or time. These come to the mind when it's quiet but not fully established in its object. To get rid of them, reestablish mindfulness by breathing deeply into the heart three or four times, and they'll go away. If the vision is of another person, first spread goodwill to that person, and then breathe deeply into the heart to let the vision disband. **A sense of having left the body.** If you sense that you're outside your body, you may feel tempted to travel around a bit on the astral plane, but you should resist the temptation. There are dangers there, and meanwhile you're leaving your body unprotected. You can get back into the body by calling to mind the four basic properties that make up your sense of the body as felt from within: the breath energy, warmth, coolness, and solidity (see the discussion of the Fourth Jhana, in Part Four). **External presences.** If you sense an energy or unbodied presence outside your body, you don't have to figure out who it is or what's causing it. Simply fill your own body with awareness and breath energy. Think of both your awareness and your breath energy as being solid and impenetrable, from the top of the head to the tips of your fingers and toes. When you've secured your body in this way, you can spread thoughts of goodwill in the direction of the external presence and then in all directions. Keep this up until the sense of the external presence goes away.

## GETTING STUCK ON CONCENTRATION

There are two types of attachment to concentration: healthy and unhealthy. Healthy attachment to concentration is a necessary element in developing it as a skill. With this kind of attachment you try to maintain your inner stillness in all situations as you fulfill your other responsibilities throughout the day. You take an interest in figuring out why you can't maintain it in some situations, and try to find free time to devote to more formal practice, even if it's only little meditation breaks throughout the day. The reason this attachment is healthy is because it helps you to recognize any unhealthy attachment as a problem to be solved, and it gives you a good home base from which to solve it.

With unhealthy attachment to concentration, you don't want to leave formal practice at all, don't want to engage with other people at all, and don't want to fulfill your responsibilities in the world, for you see that the world is nothing but a disturbance to your peace of mind. You simply want to use the concentration as an excuse to run away from your responsibilities in the world.

You have to remember that your responsibilities are important opportunities for you to develop the good qualities you'll need to train the mind in discernment: Patience. Persistence. Equanimity. Also, the turmoil you sense in dealing with the world doesn't come from the world; it comes from within your own mind. If you simply hide out in concentration, you'll curl up around the sources of your inner turmoil and never be able to uproot them. Eventually, they'll destroy your concentration and you won't have anything to hold onto at all.

### RANDOM INSIGHTS

If an insight suddenly pops into your head while you're meditating, you have to decide quickly whether it's something worth paying attention to or simply another distraction. A quick rule of thumb is this: If the insight can be applied directly to what you're doing right then and there in your meditation, go ahead and give it a try. See how it works. If it doesn't work, drop it. If it doesn't apply directly to what you're doing, drop it. Don't be afraid that you'll lose something valuable. If you try to hold onto it, it'll lead you further and further away from the breath. If it's really valuable, it'll stick in your mind without your trying to remember it.

Think of concentration as a goose that lays golden eggs. If you spend all your time gathering and storing the eggs, the goose will die from lack of attention. And the gold of these eggs is like the gold in most fairy tales: If you don't put it to good use right away, it'll turn into feathers and ashes. So if the egg can't be used right away, discard it. Put your energy into looking after the goose.

This is another area where it's important to remember: Not everything that pops into a quiet mind is reliable. Quieting the mind gives you access to many rooms in the mind that you might have closed off in the past, but just because the rooms are now open doesn't mean that they all contain valuables. Some of them hold nothing but old junk.

If an insight that you put aside during the meditation still comes to mind after your meditation, ask yourself how it applies to the way you conduct your life. If it seems to offer a wise perspective on how to act in a particular situation, you might give it a try to see if it really is helpful. Also, to make sure you don't get taken in by a one-sided insight, ask yourself: To what extent is the opposite true? This is one of the most important questions to keep on hand to maintain your balance as a meditator.

If the insight is of a more abstract sort—about the meaning of the universe or whatever—let it go. Remember that the questions of discernment deal not with abstractions but with actions. *Your* actions. The insights you're looking for in your meditation are those dealing with your actions as well.

*Additional readings:*

On dealing with pain: Ajaan MahaBoowa Ñanasampanno – *Straight from the Heart,* in particular the talks, "Feelings of Pain" and "Investigating Pain"

The talk, "A Good Dose of Dhamma," in Upasika Kee Nanayon, *An Unentangled Knowing,* also gives good pointers on dealing with pain and illness.

On having the right attitude toward mistakes: "How to Fall" in *Meditations*

*Meditations 5* contains many talks on ways of dealing with disruptive emotions.

On the uses of gratitude as a theme of contemplation: "The Lessons of Gratitude"

*Relevant talks:*

2012/5/23: PAIN IS NOT THE ENEMY
2012/7/31: PLEASURE & PAIN
2010/6/5: INSIGHT INTO PAIN
2012/11/22: TAKE THE ONE SEAT
2012/1/1: STRENGTHENING CONVICTION
2010/3/23: PERCEPTIONS OF THE BREATH
2009/11/9: THE POWER OF PERCEPTION
2008/2/3: JUDGING YOUR MEDITATION
2008/2/6: GOOD & BAD MEDITATION
2012/1/12: EVALUATING YOUR PRACTICE
2010/11/28: MEASURING PROGRESS
2010/11/19: DELUSION CONCENTRATION
2003/1: NO MISTAKES ARE FATAL
2009/10/3: UPS & DOWNS
2009/7/26: PATIENCE & URGENCY
2012/8/10: FABRICATING WITH AWARENESS
2012/8/17: THE ARROW IN THE HEART
2004/11/24: UNSKILLFUL THINKING
2011/4/14: UNLEARNING UNSKILLFUL BEHAVIOR
2010/4/21: THE ARROWS OF EMOTION
2012/7/22: A REFUGE FROM ILLNESS, AGING, & DEATH
2011/1/30: SOBER UP
2011/10/20: IN THE MOOD
2011/8/15: TODAY IS BETTER THAN YESTERDAY
2010/12/7: GET OUT OF THE WAY
2010/12/13: ANTIDOTES
2010/11/11: SORTING YOURSELVES OUT
2005/3/9: PURITY OF HEART
2012/7/25: FEEDING ON THE BREATH
2012/7/27: PRACTICING FROM GRATITUDE

PART THREE

# Meditation in Daily Life

There are two main reasons for extending meditation practice into daily life. The first is that you create a momentum that carries through from one session of formal practice to the next. If you chop up your life into times when you meditate and times when you don't, the energy built up with each meditation session dissipates in the interim. Each time you sit down to meditate, you have to start again from scratch.

It's like keeping a dog on a leash. If the dog is left on a long leash, it tends to get the leash wound around all sorts of things: lampposts, trees, people's legs. You're faced with the long, laborious process of untangling the leash to bring both the dog and the leash back to where you are. But if the dog's on a short leash, then when you sit down, the dog and the leash are right there. In the same way, if you try to maintain the center of your meditation throughout the day, then when the time comes to sit down in meditation, you're already in your center. You can continue from there.

The second reason for extending meditation practice into daily life is that it allows you to bring the skills you've developed in the meditation to bear right where they're most needed: the mind's tendency to create stress and suffering for itself throughout the day.

Having a sense of your center as a safe, comfortable place helps keep you grounded in the midst of the turmoil of daily life. You're not blown away by outside events, for you have a solid basis inside. It's like having a post at a rocky beach at the edge of a sea. If the post is simply left lying on the beach, the waves will drive it back and forth. It will be a danger to anyone who plays in the waves. Eventually, the waves will ram the post against the rocks and smash it to smithereens. But if the post is set upright and driven deep into bedrock, the waves won't be able to move it. It'll stay safe and sound, and pose no danger to anyone at all.

Some people complain that trying to practice meditation in the midst of daily life simply adds one more task to the many tasks they're already trying to juggle, but don't see it in that way. Meditation gives you a solid place to stand so that you can juggle your other responsibilities with more ease and finesse. As many meditators will tell you, the more mindfulness and alertness you bring to your responsibilities, the better your performance. Instead of interfering with your work, the meditation makes you more attentive and alert in doing it. The fact that you're staying focused, instead of letting the mind wander all over the place, helps to husband your energy, so that you can bring more stamina to whatever you have to do.

At the same time, having a clear sense of a still center helps you to see movements of the mind you otherwise would have missed. It's like lying on your back in the middle of a field. If you look up at the sky without reference to anything on the ground, you can't tell how fast the clouds are moving, or in which direction. But if you have a still point of reference—the top of a roof or a tall pole—you can clearly sense the clouds' direction and speed. In the same way, when you have a still point of reference, you can sense when the mind is heading in the wrong direction and can bring it back before it gets into trouble.

Meditation in daily life is essentially a more complicated version of walking meditation, in that you're dealing with three main areas of focus: (1) maintaining your inner focus (2) while engaged in activities (3) in the midst of the activities around you. The main differences of course are that (2) and (3) are more complex and less under your control. But there are ways to compensate for the added complexity. And you can use what measure of control you *do* have over your actions and your environment to create better conditions for your practice. All too often people try to push meditation into the cracks of their life as they're already living it, which doesn't give the meditation much room to grow. If you're really serious about treating the problem of suffering and stress, you have to rearrange your life as best you can to foster the skills you want to develop. Place the training of your mind high in your list of priorities in everything you do. The higher you can place it, the better.

As I stated in the Introduction, some of the advice given here in Part Three may assume a greater level of commitment than you're currently ready to make. So read selectively—but also in a spirit of self-honesty. Try to be clear about which members of your inner committee are making the selection.

## 1 : YOUR INNER FOCUS

You may find that you can't keep clear watch on the in-and-out breath when you're deeply involved in a complicated task, but you can maintain a general sense of the quality of the breath energy in the body.

This is an area where lessons you've learned from sitting meditation can be of help. Two skills in particular are helpful here.

1. Try to notice where the trigger points are in your breath energy field: the points that tend to tense up or tighten most quickly, leading to patterns of tension spreading into other parts of the body. Typical points are at the throat; around the heart; at the solar plexus, right in front of the stomach; or the backs of your hands or the tops of your feet.

Once you've identified a point of this sort, use that as the spot where you center your attention throughout the day. Make sure above all that the spot stays open and relaxed. If you do sense that it's tightened up, stop whatever else you're doing for a moment and breathe through it. In other words, send good breath energy into that area and allow it to relax as soon as you can. That will help disperse the power of the tension before it takes over other parts of your body and mind.

In the beginning, you may find yourself wandering away from your spot more than you're staying with it. As with the sitting meditation, you have to be patient but firm with yourself. Each time you realize that you've lost your spot, come right back to it and release any tension that's developed in the meantime. You might find it useful to set reminders for yourself: for instance, that you'll make a special effort to be in your spot each time you cross a road or come to a red light. Over time, you can set your goals higher and aim at longer stretches of time where you're centered and relaxed.

You'll be fighting some old subconscious defensive habits as you do this, so it may take time to master this skill. But if you persist in keeping your spot relaxed, you'll find that you carry less tension throughout the day. You'll be less burdened with the sense that you've got something you need to get out of your system. At the same time, you'll gain more enjoyment out of trying to maintain your center because you feel more stable and at ease. This helps to keep you with it. If you find yourself in a situation where you're simply sitting with nothing much to do—as in a meeting or a doctor's waiting room—you can bliss out on the feeling of ease in your center, and no one else will have to know.

Keeping your center spot relaxed also helps make you more sensitive to the little things that trigger you. This gives you more insight into the workings of your own mind. You gain a place where you can step back from your thoughts and watch them simply as members of the committee. You don't have to take up everything the committee proposes. If something unskillful is brought to the floor, you learn to recognize it as unskillful and breathe right through it.

As you strengthen your ability to keep your center spot relaxed and full in all situations, you're developing a foundation for your inner observer. Developing this identity in the mind helps you to go through the day with less emotional expense, and to notice things in yourself and in your surroundings that you never noticed before. In other words, it's a good foundation for discernment to arise in the course of your daily activities. It also strengthens the discernment you bring to your formal meditation.

2. The second useful breath-skill as you go through the day is to fill your body with breath and awareness when you're in a difficult situation, and especially when you're confronted with a difficult person. Think of the breath as a protective shield, so that the other person's energy doesn't penetrate yours. At the same time, visualize that person's words and actions as going past you, and not as coming straight at you. This helps you feel less threatened, and enables you to think more clearly about how to respond in an appropriate way. And because you're creating a force field of good solid energy, you might have a calming and stabilizing effect on the people and the situation around you.

This is also a good skill to master when you're dealing with people who come to tell you their troubles. All too often, we subconsciously feel that if we don't absorb some of their pain, we're not being empathetic. But our sense of absorbing their energy doesn't really lighten their load; it simply weighs us down. You can still be empathetic—and even see their problems more clearly—if you stay inside a clear cocoon of good breath energy. That way you don't confuse their pain with yours.

Ideally, you want to combine these two breath-skills into one, as you would in walking meditation. In other words, keep your focus on your chosen spot as your default mode, but learn how to expand the breath and the awareness from that spot to fill the whole body as quickly as possible whenever you feel the need. That way you're prepared for whatever comes up in the course of the day.

## II : YOUR ACTIVITIES

You'll quickly discover that the things disturbing your meditation in daily life don't all come from outside. Your own activities—what you do, say, and think—can also throw you off-balance. This is why the principle of restraint is an essential part of the practice: You make a point of refraining from doing things and directing your attention in ways that will undo the work of your meditation.

It's important *not* to think of restraint as confinement, restricting the range of your activities. Actually, it's a door to freedom—freedom from the damage you do to yourself and the people around you. Although some of the traditional forms of restraint may seem confining at first, remember that only the unskillful members of the committee are feeling hemmed in. The skillful ones who have been trampled underfoot are actually being given some space and freedom to develop and grow.

At the same time, the practice of restraint doesn't mean restricting the range of your awareness. All too often, when we think of doing something or looking at something, we focus simply on what we like or dislike. Restraint forces you to look at *why* you like or dislike things, and at *what happens as a result* when you follow your likes and dislikes. In this way, you broaden your perspective and gain insight into areas of the mind that otherwise would stay hidden behind the scenes. Restraint is thus a way of developing discernment.

Some members of the mind's committee like to argue that you'll understand them only when you give in to them, and that if you don't give in to them, they'll go underground where you can't see them. If you fall for that argument, you'll never be free of their influence. The only way around it is to be persistent in refusing to believe it, for then you get to see their next line of defense, and then the next. Finally you'll come to the level where they reveal themselves, and you'll see how weak their reasoning really is. So here again, restraint is a way of developing discernment into areas that indulgence keeps hidden.

Another way of thinking about restraint is to regard meditation as an exercise in developing a home for the mind—a place inside where you can rest with a sense of protection and gather nourishment for the mind. If you lack restraint, it's as if the windows and doors of your inner home were open 24 hours a day. People and animals can come and go and leave whatever mess they want. If you close your windows and doors only when you practice formal meditation, you get forced into the role of a janitor each time you start to meditate. And you'll find that some of the people or animals that have wandered into your home won't be willing to leave. They'll eat up all the nourishment you've gathered, and you won't have any left for yourself. So you have to gain a sense of discernment as to when you should open and close your windows and doors. That way your mind will have a good home.

If you're afraid that restraint will deprive you of your spontaneity, remember the harm that untrained spontaneity can cause. Think of the things that you said or did on the spur of the moment that you then regretted for a long time afterwards. What you thought was your "natural spontaneity" was simply the force of an unskillful habit, as artificial and contrived as any other habit. Spontaneity becomes admirable and "in the zone" only when it has been trained to the point where skillful action becomes effortless. This is what we admire in the greatest artists, performers, and sports stars. Their spontaneity required years of training. So look at restraint as a way of training your spontaneity to become effortlessly skillful. This may take time, but it's time well spent.

There are three traditional ways of exercising restraint: developing a sense of moderation in your conversation, following precepts, and exercising restraint over your senses.

## MODERATION IN CONVERSATION

Lesson number one in meditation is keeping control of your mouth. If you can't control your mouth there's no way you're going to control your mind.

So, before you say anything, ask yourself: (1) "Is this true?" (2) "Is this beneficial?" (3) "Is this the right time to say this?" If the answer to all three questions is Yes, then go ahead and say it. If not, then keep quiet.

When you make a habit of asking yourself these questions, you find that very little conversation is really worthwhile.

This doesn't mean that you have to become unsociable. If you're at work and you need to talk to your fellow workers to create a harmonious atmosphere in the workplace, that counts as worthwhile speech. Just be careful that social-grease speech doesn't go beyond that and turn into idle chatter. This is not only a waste of energy but also a source of danger. Too much grease can gum up the works. Often the words that cause the most harm are those that, when they pop into the mind, are allowed to go unfiltered right out the mouth.

If observing the principle of moderation in conversation means that you gain a reputation for being a quiet person, well, that's fine. You find that your words, if you're more careful about doling them out, start taking on more worth. At the same time, you're creating a better atmosphere for your mind. If you're constantly chattering all day long, how are you going to stop the mental chatter when you sit down to meditate? But if you develop the habit of watching over your mouth, the same habit comes to apply to the meditation. Your committee members all start learning to watch over their mouths as well.

This doesn't mean that you have to give up humor, just that you learn to employ humor wisely. Humor in our society tends to fall into the categories of wrong speech: falsehoods, divisive speech, coarse speech, and idle chatter. There's a challenge in learning to use your humor to state things that are true, that lead to harmony, and actually serve a good purpose. But think for a moment of all the great humorists of the past: We remember their humor because of the clever ways they expressed the truth. You may or may not aspire to be a great humorist, but the effort spent in trying to use humor wisely is a good exercise in discernment. If you can learn to laugh wisely and in a good-natured way about the foibles of the world around you, you can learn to laugh in the same way at your own foibles. And that's one of the most essential skills in any meditator's repertoire.

## PRECEPTS

A precept is a promise you make to yourself to avoid harmful behavior. No one is forcing it on you, but wise people have found that five precepts in particular are very helpful in creating a good environment for training the mind. When you take on these five precepts, you establish the resolve not to intentionally engage in five activities:

1) Killing any person or animal
2) Stealing (i.e., taking something belonging to someone else without that person's permission)
3) Having illicit sex (i.e., with a minor or with an adult who is already in another relationship or when *you* are already in another relationship)
4) Telling falsehoods (i.e., misrepresenting the truth)
5) Taking intoxicants

These precepts are designed to counteract some of the blatant ways in which your actions create disturbances, inside and out, that make it difficult to maintain your inner focus. Outside, they protect you from the sorts of actions that will lead to retaliation from others. Inside, they protect you from the two attitudes with which you can wound yourself when you know you've harmed yourself or others: low self-esteem or defensively high self-esteem.

These two forms of unhealthy self-esteem relate to the two ways people tend to react to their own misbehavior: You either (1) regret the actions or (2) engage in one of two kinds of denial, either (a) denying that your actions did in fact happen or (b) denying that they really were wrong. These reactions are like wounds in the mind. Regret is an open wound, tender to the touch, whereas denial is like hardened, twisted scar tissue around a tender spot. When the mind is wounded in these ways, it can't settle down comfortably in the present, for it finds itself resting on raw, exposed flesh or calcified knots. When it's forced to stay in the present, it's there only in a tensed, contorted, and partial way. The insights it gains tend to be contorted and partial as well. Only if the mind is free of wounds and scars can it settle down comfortably and freely in the present, and give rise to undistorted discernment.

This is where the five precepts come in: They're designed to heal these wounds and scars. They're an integral part of the healing process of meditation. Healthy self-esteem comes from living up to a set of standards that are practical, clear-cut, humane, and worthy of respect. The five precepts are formulated in such a way that they provide just such a set of standards.

• *Practical:* The standards set by the precepts are simple. You promise yourself not to engage intentionally in any of the five kinds of harmful activities, and not to tell anyone else to engage in them, either. That's all. You don't have to worry about controlling more than that. This means that the precepts don't require you to focus on indirect or unintended ways in which your actions may lead to someone else's breaking the precepts. You focus first on your own choices to act.

If, after time, you want to expand your promises to yourself to avoid behavior that might indirectly cause others to break the precepts—such as buying meat—that's entirely up to you. But in the beginning, it's wisest to focus on what you yourself choose to do, for that's an area where you can exert true control.

It's entirely possible to live in line with these standards—not always easy or convenient, maybe, but always possible. Some of the precepts may be easier for you to keep than others, but with time and patience—and a little wisdom in dealing with lapses in your behavior—they become more and more manageable. This is especially true when you start noticing the benefits that come from keeping them, and the harm that's caused when you lapse.

Some people translate the precepts into standards that sound more lofty or noble—taking the second precept, for example, to mean no abuse of the planet's resources—but even those who reformulate the precepts in this way admit that it's impossible to live up to them. Anyone who has suffered from having to live up to impossible standards can tell you of the psychological damage such standards can cause. If you can give yourself standards that take a little effort and mindfulness but are possible to meet, your self-esteem soars dramatically as you discover within yourself the ability to meet those standards. You can then face more demanding tasks with confidence.

• *Clear-cut:* The precepts are formulated with no ifs, ands, or buts. This means that they give very clear guidance, with no room for waffling or less-than-honest rationalizations. An action either fits in with the precepts or it doesn't. Again, standards of this sort are very healthy to live by. Anyone who has raised children has found that, although children may complain about hard and fast rules, they actually feel more secure with them than with rules that are vague and always open to negotiation. Clear-cut rules don't allow for unspoken agendas to come sneaking in the back door of the mind. When, through training yourself in rules like this, you learn that you can trust your motivations, you gain a genuinely healthy sense of self-esteem. At the same time, holding to a clear-cut rule saves you the time you might otherwise waste in trying to blur the line and justify unskillful behavior to yourself.

• *Humane:* The precepts are humane both to the person who observes them and to the people affected by his or her actions. If you observe them, you're aligning yourself with a humane principle: that the most important powers shaping your experience of the world are the intentional thoughts, words, and deeds you choose in the present moment. This means that you are not insignificant. With every choice you make—at home, at work, at play—you are exercising your power in the ongoing fashioning of the world. Keeping the precepts ensures that your contribution to the world is always positive.

As for your effect on other people: If you follow the precepts, your contribution to the world is in line with the principles of goodwill and compassion. This helps you to develop the brahmaviharas with no fear of hypocrisy or denial.

• *Worthy of respect:* The five precepts are called "standards appealing to the noble ones"—people who have gained at least the first taste of awakening. Such people don't accept standards simply on the basis of popularity. They've put their lives on the line to see what leads to true happiness and have seen for themselves, for example, that all lying is pathological, and that sex in violation of a committed relationship is unsafe at any speed. Other people may not respect you for living by the five precepts, but noble ones do, and their respect is worth more than that of anyone else in the world.

Some people are afraid of keeping the precepts for fear of becoming proud that their behavior is better than other people's. This sort of pride, however, is easy to drop when you remember that you're observing the precepts not to make yourself better than others, but simply to cure the problems in your own mind. It's like taking medicine: If you take your medicine when other people are not taking theirs, that's no reason to look down on them. You may encourage them to take their health more seriously, but if they refuse to heed your encouragement, you have to drop the matter for the time being and concentrate on recovering your own health.

The healthy sort of pride that comes from observing the precepts focuses on comparing yourself with yourself—in other words, on the fact that you've learned how to be less harmful and more thoughtful than you used to be. This sort of pride is much better than the opposite sort: the conceit that views the precepts as petty, claiming to be above them. That sort of pride is doubly damaging: both to your mind and to the happiness of others. It's much healthier to respect yourself for submitting to a strict training and mastering it. That sort of respect is good for you and for everyone else.

In addition to creating a healthy attitude and peaceful environment conducive to the practice, the precepts exercise many of the skills you need to get started in meditation. They give you practice in setting up a skillful intention and then sticking with it. They also give you practice in dealing in a mature way with any lapses that may occur. To keep to them successfully, you have to learn how to recognize and acknowledge a mistake without getting tied up in remorse and self-recrimination. You simply reaffirm your intention not to make that slip again, and then develop the brahmaviharas to help strengthen that intention. This way you learn both how to take your mistakes in stride and how not to repeat them.

The precepts also develop the mental qualities needed specifically for concentration: *mindfulness* to keep them in mind, *alertness* to keep watch over your actions to make sure that they stay in line with your precepts, and *ardency* to anticipate situations where you might be tempted to break your precepts, so that you can plan a skillful strategy that will keep your precepts intact. This then develops your discernment.

For example, there will be situations where telling the truth about a particular topic might be harmful to others. How do you avoid talking about that topic and yet still not tell a lie? When you promise yourself not to kill, you have to anticipate that pests may invade your home. How can you keep them out without killing them?

In these ways, the precepts help to foster a conducive environment around the practice of meditation, at the same time exercising skills you need to develop within the meditation itself.

### RESTRAINT OF THE SENSES

The senses here are six: your senses of sight, hearing, smell, taste, and touch, along with the sense of ideation—your mind's knowledge of ideas. Restraint of these senses doesn't mean going around with blinders on your eyes or plugs in your ears. It actually forces you to see more than you normally might, for it requires you to become sensitive to two things: (1) your motivation for, say, looking at a particular sight; and (2) what's happening to your mind as a result of looking at that sight. In this way you bring the questions of discernment to bear in an area where you're usually driven by the questions of hunger: the search to see or hear delicious things. You learn to view your engagement with the senses as part of a causal process. This is how restraint helps to develop discernment. At the same time, you learn to counteract causal currents that would disturb the mind. This helps to develop concentration.

To resist getting swept away by these currents, you have to maintain your center of awareness within the body. That type of center is like an anchor for securing the mind. Then make sure that your center is comfortable. That keeps the mind well fed, so that it doesn't abandon its anchor to flow along with those currents in search of food. When the mind isn't hungry for pleasure, it'll be much more willing to exercise restraint over the currents going out the eyes, ears, nose, tongue, body, and mind. Once the mind is firmly centered, you're in a good position to step out of the currents and view them in terms of both aspects of their causal patterns.

1. Each time you direct your attention to the senses, try to be clear about your *motivation*. Realize that you're not a passive receiver of sights, sounds, etc. The mind actually goes out looking for sensory stimuli. And often it's looking for trouble. There are times, for instance, when there's nothing in your surroundings to inspire lust, but lust arises in the mind and goes looking for something to nourish itself. The same thing happens with anger and all your other emotions.

So when you look at things, what are you looking for? Who's doing the looking? Is lust doing the looking? Is anger doing the looking? If you let these emotions direct your eyes, they get used to ordering your mind around as well. You're strengthening the very committee members that you'll later need to wrestle down during the meditation.

If you see that unskillful intentions are directing where you focus your attention or how you look at something, change your focus. Look at something else, or look at the same thing in a different way. If you've been contemplating a beautiful body, look for the aspects that aren't so beautiful—and they aren't far away, just under the skin. The same principle holds for anger. If you're thinking about someone you really hate, remember that there's another side to that person as well, a good side. Be a person with two eyes, and not just one. Or if you find that when you drop the lust or the anger, you're no longer interested in looking at or thinking about those people, you realize that the problem wasn't with them. It was with the committee in your mind. You learn that you can't really trust some of its members. This is a good lesson to learn on a daily basis.

2. A similar principle applies when you take note of the *results* of your looking. If you realize that the way you've been looking at something has started to aggravate unskillful mental states, either look away or learn to look at the same thing in a way that counteracts those mental states. The same applies to what you listen to, what you smell, what you taste, what you touch, and especially what you think about.

If you can keep your attention focused on the way in which the mind initiates sensory contact and is affected by sensory contact, you're staying focused inside even as you look or listen outside. This helps to keep the center of your focus firm and resilient throughout the day.

## III : YOUR SURROUNDINGS

The values of human society, for the most part, fly right in the face of a meditative life. Either they make fun of the idea of a true, unchanging happiness, or they avoid the topic entirely, or else they say that you can't reach an unchanging happiness through your own efforts. This is true even in societies that have traditionally been Buddhist, and it's especially so in modern society, where the media exert pressure to look for happiness in things that will change. The practice of meditation for the sake of an unconditioned happiness is always counter-cultural. No one else is going to protect your conviction in the possibility of true happiness. You have to protect it yourself. So learn how to skillfully shelter your practice from the conflicting values of society at large.

There are three basic ways in which you can do this: choosing admirable friends, learning to live frugally, and finding seclusion as much as you can.

These three issues require a fair amount of renunciation, and renunciation is easiest when you regard it not as deprivation but as a trade. In trading the pleasures of an ordinary life for a meditative life, you're trading candy for gold. Or you may think of yourself as an athlete in training. The game of outwitting your unskillful habits is far more worthwhile than any sport. Just as athletes are willing to live under certain restrictions for the sake of their performance, you should be willing to live under certain restrictions for the sake of true happiness. And just as an athlete restricted to a healthy diet comes to prefer healthy food to junk food, you often find that the restrictions you place on the way you interact with your surroundings actually become your preferred mode of being.

## ADMIRABLE FRIENDS

When you associate with a person, you unconsciously pick up that person's habits and views. This is why the most important principle in shaping the environment around your daily meditation is to associate with admirable people.

Admirable people have four qualities: They're virtuous, generous, wise, and have conviction in the principle that skillful qualities should be developed, and unskillful qualities abandoned. If you can find people like this, try to associate with them. Notice their good qualities, try to emulate them, and ask them how you might develop more virtue, generosity, wisdom, and conviction yourself.

So look around you. If you don't see any people like this, search them out.

The problem is, what to do with the people around you who aren't admirable, but with whom you have to spend time at home, at work, or at social occasions. This issue is especially difficult if they're people for whom you're responsible, or to whom you have debts of gratitude, such as your parents. You have to spend time with these people; you have to help them. So learn what it means to spend time with people without associating with them—i.e., without picking up their habits and values. The primary principle is that you don't go to them for advice on moral or spiritual issues.

Also, try to excuse yourself every time they try to pull you into activities that go against your precepts or principles. If the activities are unavoidable—as when there's a party at work—take the attitude of being an anthropologist from Mars, observing the strange habits of earthlings in this society at this point in time.

If there are people or situations that tend to bring out the worst in you, and you can't avoid them, sit down and devote a meditation session to planning how you can survive the encounter without getting your buttons pushed and with a minimum of unnecessary conflict. Learning how to prevent unskillful qualities from arising in the mind is an important part of the path, but all too often it's overlooked. Not every meditation has to focus on the present. Just make sure that planning doesn't take over your meditation and go beyond the bounds of what's really helpful.

In some cases, if a friendship is centered on unskillful activities, you might consider putting it on hold. Even though the other person's feelings might be hurt, you have to ask yourself which is more precious: that person's feelings or the state of your mind. (And remember: Simply hurting another person's feelings is not the same thing as causing that person harm.) You'll eventually have more to offer that person—if you practice seriously, you can become that person's admirable friend—so don't think of your pulling away as an unkind act.

If your friends are concerned that you're becoming less social, talk the issue over with someone you trust.

The principle of being selective with your friends applies not only to people in the flesh, but also to the media: newspapers, magazines, television, radio, internet, internet, internet. Here it's easier to turn things off without compunction. If you do feel the need to spend time with the media, ask yourself each time: Why am I doing this? What kind of people will I be associating with when I do? When they say something, why do they want me to believe it? Can I trust them? Who are their sponsors?

Even reading/watching the news has its dangers for someone training the mind. There's nothing wrong with trying to stay informed of current events, but you have to be sensitive to the effect that too much attention to the news can have on your mind. The basic message of the news is that your time is unimportant, that the important things in the world are what other people are doing in other places. This is the opposite of the message of meditation: that the most important thing happening in your world is what you're doing right here, right now.

So exercise moderation even in the amount of news you watch. Instead, watch the news being made right at your breath. And when you have news of this sort to report, report it only to people who have earned your trust.

## FRUGALITY

Buddhist monks are encouraged every day to reflect on why they use the four requisites of life: food, clothing, shelter, and medicine. The purpose of this reflection is to see if they've been using these things to excess or in ways that will develop unskillful states of mind. They're also advised to reflect on the fact that each of the requisites has come about through the sacrifices of many, many people and other living beings. This reflection encourages the monks to live simply and to aim ultimately at a truly noble form of happiness that places no burdens on anyone at all.

Lay meditators benefit from reflecting daily in this way as well, to counteract the way society at large encourages you to focus your attention on consumption and acquisition with no thought for the consequences. So stop to think, for example, when you eat: Is it just to keep yourself strong enough to fulfill your duties? Or are you, in the words of the Buddhist texts, searching out the tip-top tastes with the tip of your tongue? Are you bulking up just to look good? If so, you're fostering unskillful states of mind. Are you too picky about what kinds of food you will and won't eat? If so, you're spending too much time and money on your eating—time and money that could be used to develop generosity or other skillful mental states.

You have to realize that in eating—even if it's vegetarian food—you're placing a burden on the world around you, so you want to give some thought to the purposes served by the strength you gain from your food. Don't eat just for the fun of it, because the beings—human and animal—who provided the food didn't provide it in fun. Make sure the energy gets put to good use.

This doesn't mean, however, that you should starve yourself. Starving yourself to look good is also unskillful, in that it drains away the energy you need to practice, and keeps you inordinately fastened on the appearance of the body. The traditional term for wise eating is *moderation* in eating: having a sense of just right, of exactly how much is needed to keep you healthy and strong enough to stick with the training of the mind.

The same principle holds true for the other requisites. You don't want to be a miser, but at the same time you don't want to waste the resources that you or someone you depend on worked so hard to acquire. Don't be a slave to style. Don't take more from the world than you're willing to give back. And learn to undo the perceptions—so heavily promoted by the media—that shopping is a form of therapy and that a purchase is nothing but a victory or a gain. Every purchase also entails loss. To begin with, there's the loss of money that could be used to develop skillful qualities of mind—such as generosity—rather than unskillful qualities, like greed. Then there's a loss of freedom. All too often, the things you own begin to own you. The more things you own, the more you have to fear from the dangers that can come to things, such as theft, fire, and flood. So learn to restrict your purchases to things that really are useful, and use the money you save to help advance the higher qualities of life, both for yourself and for those around you. Think of frugality as a gift both to yourself and to the world.

## SECLUSION

Seclusion enables you to look directly at the issues created by your own mind without the distraction of issues created by other people. It's a chance to get in touch with yourself and to reaffirm your true values. This is why the Buddha advised monks to go into the wilderness, and to create a wilderness state of mind even when living in society.

There are several ways you can create that state of mind in your life.

**Chanting.** To foster a sense of seclusion around your daily meditation session, you might find it helpful to chant before you meditate. This is especially helpful if you notice that your mind is carrying a lot of issues from the day. The sound of the chanting is calming, and the words of the chanting help to put you in a new frame of mind. There are many chanting texts available on-line, and many sound files showing how to pronounce the words. It's possible to chant in any of the Asian Buddhist languages, in your own language, or a combination of both. Experiment to see which style of chanting is most effective for putting you in the best frame of mind to meditate.

**Retreats.** In addition to your daily meditation session, it's helpful to find times at regular intervals when you can set aside longer periods of time for meditation practice. This allows you to go deeper into your mind and to recharge your practice in general. There are two ways you can do this, and it's useful to try both. The first is to find time on a regular basis every week or two to devote a larger part of the day than you normally do for the practice. The second is to go on an extended retreat once or twice a year.

• Traditionally, Buddhists set aside four days out of the month—the full-moon day, the new-moon day, and the two half-moon days—for more earnest practice. This is called observing the *uposatha (oo-PO-sa-ta)*. The most common way of observing the uposatha involves taking the eight precepts, listening to the Dhamma (the Buddha's teachings), and meditating.

The eight precepts build on the five. The third precept is changed from no illicit sex to no sex at all. With the remaining three precepts you promise yourself that for the duration of the day you'll refrain from:

6) Eating food during the period from noon until the following dawn

7) Watching shows, listening to music, using jewelry, cosmetics, and scents

8) Sitting on high, luxurious seats or lying on high, luxurious beds

These precepts essentially add the principle of restraint of the senses to the five precepts. Because they place limits on the pleasure you try to take from each of the five physical senses, they encourage you to examine your attachment to the body and to sensual pleasures, and to look for pleasure in training your mind instead.

To listen to the Buddha's teachings, you can read a Dhamma book aloud or listen to any of the good Dhamma talks available online.

Of course, you can adjust these observances as fits your schedule. For instance, you can vary the number of times you attempt them in one month. You can schedule them for days you're normally off work. If you can't eat before noon, you can simply promise yourself that you won't eat food after the mid-day meal.

If you have friends who are meditators, you might try scheduling an uposatha day together to see if the energy of the group helps or hinders your practice. Although it may seem strange to seek seclusion in the company of others, you may find that it makes the practice feel less lonely, for you can see that you're not the only person bucking the values of society at large. To help foster an atmosphere of seclusion in the group, agree on the amount of conversation you want to engage in. Avoid discussions of politics. Generally, the more silence, the better. You're not meeting to teach one another through words. You're meeting to teach and support one another through example.

• As for extended retreats, there are many meditation centers offering retreats throughout the year. The advantage of centers like these is that they tend to enforce a set group schedule, which helps to structure your day. This can be important if you're just getting started with meditation and have trouble being a self-starter. Also, the work schedule tends to be minimal. Your food will be cooked for you, so you'll have more time for formal meditation.

However, you have to be careful in choosing a good center. Many are run as businesses with sizable staffs. This drives the fees up and drives the Dhamma away from what the Buddha taught and in the direction of what pleases a large clientele. Some centers will apply subtle pressure at the end of the retreat for you to give a donation to the center or the teacher(s) of the retreat, claiming that this is an ancient Buddhist custom. The tradition of giving donations is a Buddhist custom; the tradition of applying pressure for donations is not.

If the Dhamma taught on the retreat goes against what you know is true, avoid the Dhamma talks and meditate someplace else in the center. If you're not sure, meditate during the Dhamma talks, giving all your attention to your meditation theme. If anything in the talk is relevant or helpful to what you're doing, it will come right to your attention. As for everything else, you can let it pass.

Even the centers run on a donation basis can teach very strange versions of the Dhamma. If you sense anything of a cultish atmosphere at a center, leave immediately. If they refuse to let you leave, make a scene. Remember, you have to protect your mind.

Meditation monasteries are another alternative. They charge no fees, as everything is run on a donation basis. But because you will be expected to help with the daily chores, you may have less time for formal meditation. Also, meditation monasteries often don't have set group schedules, so you'll have to be more of a self-starter. And even here, you have to be discriminating in how you listen to the Dhamma.

You can also search the internet for centers that allow you to rent a small cabin to meditate on your own.

Another alternative is to go camping. In the United States, state and national forests and federal BLM (Bureau of Land Management) land tend to provide more opportunities for seclusion than state and national parks, as they don't force you to stay in campgrounds. Being in the wilderness also helps to put many of the issues of your daily life into a larger perspective. There's a reason why the Buddha went into the wilderness to gain awakening.

*Additional readings:*

For some general perspectives on practice in daily life: "Skills to Take with You" in *Meditations;* "A Meditative Life" in *Meditations2*

On using the breath in difficult social situations: "Social Anxiety" in *Meditations3*

On controlling your mouth: "Right Speech"

On examining your intentions: "The Road to Nirvana is Paved with Skillful Intentions"

On the etiquette of generosity, both for those who give and for those who receive: "No Strings Attached"

On renunciation and uposatha practice: "The Dignity of Restraint" in *Meditations;* "Trading Candy for Gold"

On forgiveness: "Reconciliation, Right & Wrong"

On some of the issues encountered in following the precepts: "Getting the Message"; "Educating Compassion"; "The Healing Power of the Precepts"

*Relevant talks:*

2011/6/20: FOR THE SURVIVAL OF YOUR GOODNESS
2011/10/22: AFTER-WORK MEDITATION
2009/8/14: A CULTURE OF SELF-RELIANCE
2006/10/13: A WILDERNESS MIND AT HOME
2010/8/25: SKILLS TO TAKE HOME
2001/8: NEW FEEDING HABITS
2007/12/20: THE SKILL OF RESTRAINT
2011/8/12: RIGHT SPEECH, INSIDE & OUT
2012/4/16: A MEDITATOR IS A GOOD FRIEND TO HAVE
2010/12/10: THE IVORY INTERSECTION
2009/1/23: CARING WITHOUT CLINGING
2011/5/12: PROTECTING YOUR SPACE
2008/5/28: AN ANTHROPOLOGIST FROM MARS
2005/3/16: RENUNCIATION

PART FOUR

# *Advanced Practice*

Breath meditation is an ideal practice for giving rise to strong states of concentration, called jhana. Jhana then provides an ideal basis for fostering the insights that can free the mind from its habitual ways of causing itself suffering and stress. Those insights can ultimately lead to an experience of release into the unconditioned dimension—called the deathless—where suffering and stress all end. So there are three aspects to advanced practice: jhana, insight, and release.

## JHANA

The Pali Canon describes four levels of jhana, and five formless attainments—states of concentration in which there is no experience of the form of the body—that take the fourth jhana as their point of departure. Texts drawing on the Pali Canon have mapped out these descriptions, listing the factors that go into each jhana or formless attainment.

It's important when reading these lists to realize that they're not recipes. For instance, you can't simply take the five factors of the first jhana, combine them, and then expect to get the first jhana. That would be like hearing that the tropical fruit durian smells like custard combined with garlic, and that it contains a little cyanide, some vitamin E, and a large dose of potassium. If you simply combined these ingredients in hopes of getting durian, you'd actually get a poisonous mess.

The lists of jhana factors are more like restaurant reviews. They tell you what a successful version of a particular dish should or shouldn't taste like, but they don't give many clues on how to make that dish yourself.

So to get the most out of the restaurant reviews, you can combine them with a recipe to give you a fuller idea of how the recipe should work. That's what's offered here. The basic recipe for jhana is given in Parts One and Two of this book. When you focus on the breath following the recipe, and things begin to go well, these are some of the experiences you can expect.

**The first jhana.** Traditionally, the first jhana has five factors: directed thought, evaluation, singleness of preoccupation (the theme you're focused on), rapture, and pleasure. The first three factors are the causes; the last two, the results. In other words, you don't *do* rapture and pleasure. They come about when you do the first three factors well.

In this case, *directed thought* means that you keep directing your thoughts to the breath. You don't direct them anywhere else. This is the factor that helps you stay concentrated on one thing.

*Evaluation* is the discernment factor, and it covers several activities. You evaluate how comfortable the breath is, and how well you're staying with the breath. You think up ways of improving either your breath or the way you're focused on the breath; then you try them out, evaluating the results of your experiments. If they don't turn out well, you try to think up new approaches. If they do turn out well, you try to figure out how to get the most out of them. This last aspect of evaluation includes the act of spreading good breath energy into different parts of the body, spreading your awareness to fill the body as well, and then maintaining that sense of full-body breath and full-body awareness.

Evaluation also plays a role in fighting off any wandering thoughts that might arise: It quickly assesses the damage that would come to your concentration if you followed such thoughts, and reminds you of why you want to come back on topic. When the meditation is going well, evaluation has less work to do in this area and can focus more directly on the breath and the quality of your focus on the breath.

In short, evaluation plays both a passive and an active role in your relation to the breath. Its passive role is simply stepping back to watch how things are going. In this role, it develops both your alertness and your inner *observer*, which I discussed in Part One. The active role of evaluation is to pass judgment on what you've observed and to figure out what to do with it. If you judge that the results of your mental actions aren't satisfactory, you try to find ways to change what you're doing, and then put your ideas to the test. If the results *are* satisfactory, you figure out ways to maintain them and put them to good use. This develops your inner *doer* so that it can be more skillful in shaping the state of your mind.

*Singleness of preoccupation* means two things: First, it refers to the fact that your directed thought and evaluation both stay with nothing but the breath. In other words, your preoccupation is single in the sense that it's the one thing you're focused on. Second, your preoccupation is single in the sense that one thing— the breath—fills your awareness. You may be able to hear sounds outside the body, but your attention doesn't run to them. They're totally in the background. (This point applies to all the jhanas, and can even apply to the formless attainments, although some people, on reaching the formless attainments, find that they don't hear sounds.)

When these three factors are solid and skillful, *rapture* and *pleasure* arise. The word "rapture" here is a translation of a Pali word—*piti*—that can also mean refreshment. It's basically a form of energy and can be experienced in many ways: either as a quiet, still fullness in body and mind; or else as a moving energy, such as a thrill running through the body or waves washing over you. Sometimes it will cause the body to move. With some people, the experience is intense; for others, it's gentler. This can, in part, be determined by how much your body is hungering for the energy. If it's really hungry, the experience will be intense. If not, the experience may hardly be noticeable.

As I noted in Part Two, most people find the rapture pleasant, but some find it unpleasant. In either case, the important point is not to focus on it, but to stay focused on the breath. Let the rapture move any way it likes. You don't have to try to control it. Otherwise, you drop the causal factors—directed thought, evaluation, and singleness of preoccupation—and your concentration unravels.

Pleasure is the sense of ease and well-being that come when the body feels soothed by the breath, and the mind is pleasurably interested in the work of the meditation. Here again it's important to stay focused on the breath and not to focus on the pleasure, for that would lose touch with the causes of the concentration.

Instead, use your awareness of the breath and your powers of evaluation to allow—that's the operative word: *allow*—the feelings of rapture and pleasure to fill the body. When rapture and pleasure totally interpenetrate the body, they strengthen the singleness of your preoccupation with the whole-body breath.

In this way, the activity of evaluation, instead of being an unfortunate unsteadiness in your concentration, actually strengthens it, so that the mind is ready to settle down more securely.

As you work with the breath in this way, you'll notice that your awareness of the body has two aspects: focused awareness and the background awareness already in your body. The background awareness is simply your receptivity to the full range of sensory input coming in from all the parts of the body. The focused awareness is located at the spot where you're paying special attention to that input and developing it further. One of the jobs of your evaluation is to get these two aspects of awareness in touch with each other. The background awareness is already there, just like the background breath energy in the body. The question—both with the background awareness and with the background energy—is: Is it full? Remember that, when dealing with the breath, you're not trying forcefully to pump breath into areas where it's never been before. You're simply allowing all the aspects of breath energy to connect. The connectedness is what allows them all to become full. The same principle applies to your awareness: You're not trying to create new awareness. You want your focused awareness simply to connect with your background awareness so that they form a solid, fully alert whole.

As both the breath and the awareness come together in this way, you enter the second jhana.

**The second jhana** has three factors: singleness of preoccupation, rapture, and pleasure. As the breath and awareness become one, they begin to feel saturated. No matter how much you try to make them feel even more full, they can't fill any further. At this point, directed thought and evaluation have no further work to do. You can let them go. This allows the mind to enter an even stronger sense of oneness. Your focused awareness and your background awareness become firmly one, and they in turn become one with the breath.

It's as if, in the first jhana, you were identifying with one part of your breath and one part of your awareness as you worked another part of the breath through another part of your awareness. Now those dividing lines are erased. Awareness becomes one, the breath becomes one, and both become one with each other. Another analogy is to think of the mind as the lens of a camera. In first jhana, the focal point is located in front of the lens. In the second, it moves into the lens itself. This sense of oneness is maintained through all the remaining jhanas and formless states up through the level known as the dimension of the infinitude of consciousness (see below).

Here in the second jhana, both the pleasure and the rapture become more prominent, but there's no need to consciously spread them through the body. They spread on their own. The rapture, though, is a moving energy. Although it may feel extremely refreshing to begin with, it can ultimately become tiresome. When that happens, try to refine the focus of your attention to a level of breath energy that's not affected by the movements of rapture. You might think of it as tuning your radio from one station playing loud music to another playing softer music. Even though the radio waves of both stations can exist in the same place, the act of tuning-in to one enables you to tune-out the other.

When you can stay with that more refined level of energy, you enter the third jhana.

The third jhana has two factors: singleness of preoccupation and pleasure. The sense of pleasure here feels very still in the body. As it fills the body, there's no sense that you're filling the body with moving breath energy. Instead, you're allowing the body to be filled with a solid, still energy. People have also described this breath as "resilient" or "steely." There is still a subtle sense of the flow of the breath around the edges of the body, but it feels like the movement of water vapor around an ice cube, surrounding the ice but not causing it to expand or contract. Because the mind doesn't have to deal with the movement of the breath energy, it can grow more settled and still. It too becomes more solid and equanimous in the presence of the bodily pleasure.

As the mind gets even more centered and still in this way, it enters the fourth jhana.

The fourth jhana has two factors: singleness of preoccupation and equanimity. At this point, even the subtle movement of the in-and-out breath falls still. There are no waves or gaps in the breath energy. Because the mind is so still, the brain is converting less oxygen into carbon dioxide, so the chemical sensors in the brain feel no need to tell the body to breathe. The oxygen that the body absorbs passively is enough to provide for its needs. Awareness fills the body, breath fills the body, breath fills awareness: This is singleness of preoccupation in full. It's also the point in concentration practice where mindfulness becomes pure: There are no lapses in your ability to remember to stay with the breath. Because both the mind and the breath are still, equanimity becomes pure as well. The mind is at total equilibrium.

When you've learned to maintain this sense of balanced stillness in the breath, you can focus on balancing the other properties of the body as well. First balance the heat and the cold. If the body feels too warm, notice where the coolest spot in the body is. Focus on the coolness there, and then allow it to spread, just as you'd spread the still breath. Similarly, if you feel too cold, find the warmest spot in the body. After you can maintain your focus on the warmth there, allow it to spread. See if you can then bring the coolness and warmth into balance, so that the body feels just right.

Similarly with the solidity of the body: Focus on the sensations that seem heaviest or most solid in the body. Then allow that solidity to spread through the body. If the body feels too heavy, then think of the still breath making it lighter. Try to find a balance so that you feel neither too heavy nor too light.

This exercise not only makes the body more comfortable as a basis for firmer concentration, but also acquaints you with the properties that make up your inner sense of the body. As we noted in Part Two, being acquainted with these properties provides you with a useful set of tools for dealing with pain and out-of-body experiences. This exercise also gives you practice in seeing the power of your perceptions: Simply noticing and labeling a particular sensation can make it stronger.

The four jhanas focus on the same topic—the breath—but the way they relate to the breath grows progressively more refined. Once the mind reaches the fourth jhana, this can form the basis for the formless attainments. Here the relationship among the stages is reversed: All the formless attainments relate to their themes in the same way—with the equanimity and singleness of the fourth jhana—but they focus on different themes. Here we will discuss just the first four of the formless attainments, as the fifth formless attainment—the cessation of perception and feeling—lies beyond the scope of this book.

**The formless attainments.** As the mind in the fourth jhana stays with the stillness of the breath filling the body, it begins to sense that the only reason it feels a boundary or form to the body is because of the *perception* or mental image of the body's form that it's been holding to. There is no movement of the breath to confirm that perception. Instead, the body feels like a cloud of mist droplets, each droplet a sensation, but with no clear boundary to the cloud.

To reach the first formless attainment, allow the perception of the form of the body to drop away. Then focus, not on the droplets of sensation, but on the space in-between them. This space then goes out beyond the body without limit and can penetrate everything else. However, you don't try to trace it out to its limit. You simply hold in mind the perception of "infinite space" or "unlimited space." If you can stay there solidly, you reach the first formless attainment, *the dimension of the infinitude of space.* See how long you can stay with that perception.

To become adept at staying with the perception of infinite space, you can try holding to it even when you've left formal meditation. As you go through the day, replace your inner focus on the breath at a spot in the body with a focus on the perception of "space" permeating everything: your body, the space around the body, other people, the physical objects around you. Hold that perception of space in the back of your mind. Whatever's happening inside or outside your body, it's all happening in the context of that perception of space. This creates a great feeling of lightness as you go through the day. If you can maintain this perception in the midst of your daily activities, you'll have an easier time accessing it and staying steadily focused on it each time you sit down for formal meditation.

After you've become adept at staying with the perception of infinite space, you can pose the question, "What knows infinite space?" Your attention shifts to the *awareness* of the space, and you realize that the awareness, like the space, has no limits, although again you don't try to trace it out to its limits. You just stay centered where you are. (If you try asking this question before you're adept at staying with the perception of infinite space, the mind will just revert to a lower level of concentration, or may leave concentration entirely. So go back to the perception of space.) If you can stay with that perception of infinite or unlimited awareness— or simply, "knowing, knowing, knowing"—you enter the second formless attainment, *the dimension of the infinitude of consciousness*.

As with the perception of space, you can train yourself to become adept at the perception of infinite consciousness by holding to it even when you've left formal meditation. Keep in mind the perception that, whatever is happening inside you or outside you, it's all happening within the context of an all-around awareness. This, too, creates a great feeling of lightness as you go through the day, and makes it easier to settle back in with the perception of infinite awareness when you turn the mind to the practice of full concentration.

It's at this stage that your inner observer gets thrown into sharp relief. When you dropped the breath for the perception of "space," you gained a clear sense that your breath and your awareness of the breath were two separate things, and you could see precisely where and how they were separate. When you dropped the perception of "space," you could see that the awareness was separate even from space. As you carry your perception of "aware" into daily life, you can apply the same principle to everything that comes your way: Objects and events are one thing; the knowing awareness is something else.

After you've become adept at staying with the perception of infinite awareness or infinite knowing, then while you're in formal meditation you can start to take this sense of the "knower" or "observer" apart. To do this, there are two questions you can ask yourself. Either, "What is still a disturbance in this knowing?" or "What's maintaining the sense of oneness in this knowing?" You see that the answer in both cases is the perception of "knowing, knowing, knowing," or "aware, aware, aware." You drop that perception, and in so doing you drop the sense of oneness. What's left is a sense of nothingness. There's still awareness, but you're not labeling it as awareness. You're just with the sense of lightness that comes from replacing the label of "knowing" with something that feels less burdensome. The label of "knowing" requires that you make an effort to keep knowing. But the label of "nothing" allows you to put that burden down. If you can stay with that perception of, "There's nothing" or "Nothing's happening," you enter the third formless attainment, *the dimension of nothingness.*

After you've become adept at staying with the perception of "There's nothing" or "Nothing's happening," you can ask yourself if there's still any disturbance in that sense of nothingness. When you see that the disturbance is caused by the perception itself, you drop the perception. If you do this when your focus is not subtle enough, you'll revert to a lower stage of concentration. But if you can stay in the mental space left empty by the perception when it falls away, that's what you do. You can't say that there's another perception there, but because you have a nonverbal sense that you know where you are, you can't say that there's no perception, either. If you can continue staying there, you enter the fourth formless attainment, *the dimension of neither perception nor non-perception.*

**Wrong concentration.** There are several states of concentration that mimic these levels of concentration in some respects, but they are wrong concentration. This is because—unlike the levels of right concentration—their range of awareness is so narrow that it doesn't provide a basis for the arising of insight.

Two of the most common states of wrong concentration are delusion concentration and the state of non-perception. People who are adept at denial or dissociation can be prone to these states. I have also known people who mistake them for release, which is a very dangerous mistake because it blocks all further progress on the path. So it's important to recognize these states for what they are.

*Delusion concentration* we have already discussed in Part Two. It comes about when the breath gets so comfortable that your focus drifts from the breath to the sense of comfort itself, your mindfulness begins to blur, and your sense of the body and your surroundings gets lost in a pleasant haze. When you emerge, you find it hard to identify where exactly you were focused.

*The state of non-perception* comes about from making your focus extremely one-pointed and so refined that it refuses to settle on or label even the most fleeting mental objects. You drop into a state in which you lose all sense of the body, of any internal or external sounds, or of any thoughts or perceptions at all. There's just enough tiny awareness to let you know, when you emerge, that you haven't been asleep. You can stay there for many hours, and yet time passes very quickly. Two hours can seem like two minutes. You can also program yourself to come out at a particular time.

This state does have its uses—as when you're in severe pain and want some respite from it. As long as you recognize that it's not right concentration or release, the only danger is that you may decide that you like hiding out there so much that you don't want to do the work needed to go further in the practice.

**How to use the map of the jhanas.** Just as discernment requires concentration to grow, concentration requires discernment. The two qualities help each other along. So now that you have a map to the stages of concentration, you need to exercise some discernment in using it properly so that it doesn't become an obstacle to the practice. Here are a few pointers to keep in mind:

*This map presents possibilities.*

The way your concentration develops may fall clearly in line with the map, or it may not. Some people find that their concentration goes naturally from one stage to the next with no planning on their part; others find that they have to make a conscious decision to move from one stage to the next. Also, you may find that the stages of your practice may not line up precisely with those on the map. Some people, for instance, experience an extra stage between the first and the second jhana, in which directed thought falls away but there's still a modicum of evaluation. Others don't see clear steps in their progress. The mind settles down so quickly to one particular stage that they're not consciously aware of having gone through the preceding steps. It's like falling suddenly to the bottom of a well: You don't notice how many layers of brick line the side of the well. You just know that you've hit bottom.

Some of these variations are perfectly fine. However, if you find that your mind goes straight to the formless steps without first passing through the jhanas in which you have a clear sense of the whole body, back up and make an extra effort to stay with the breath and fully inhabit the body. Work particularly hard at the steps associated with the first jhana: making yourself aware of the whole body breathing, and spreading breath energy to areas where it doesn't seem to flow. This may seem less restful and quiet than the formless states, but it's necessary both for your concentration to be well grounded and for insight to arise. If the mind skips over the steps related to the body, it's simply blocking out the body and turns into concentration based on denial. Denial may shut out distractions, but it isn't conducive to clear, all-around discernment.

*Keep the map in the background of your awareness as you meditate, not in the foreground.*

Remember, the theme of your meditation is the breath, not the factors of jhana. The map can be kept in the back of your mind to be pulled out when you're faced with three kinds of choices: what to do when you can't get into a state of stillness, what to do when you're in a state of stillness but have trouble maintaining it, and what to do when you've gotten stuck in a state of stillness and don't know where to go next.

Otherwise, don't even think about the factors of jhana. Pay primary attention to the breath and allow your concentration to develop naturally from your evaluation of the breath. Try not to be like the person with a tree bearing unripe mangoes who—told that ripe mangoes aren't green and hard, they're yellow and soft— tries to ripen his mangoes by painting them yellow and squeezing them until they're soft. The result, of course, is that his mangoes never get a chance to ripen. What he should do is tend to the tree—water it, fertilize it, protect it from bugs—and the mangoes will grow yellow and soft on their own. Watching and evaluating the breath is the way you tend to the tree of your concentration.

*Don't be too quick to label a state of concentration.*

If you attain a level of concentration that seems promising, don't label it right then and there. Simply try to maintain it. Then see if you can reproduce it during your next session of meditation. If you can't, don't pay it any further attention. If you can, then label it with a mental post-it note, reminding yourself of how it feels, and what level it might correspond to on the map. Don't engrave your label in stone. As you get more familiar with the territory of your mind, you may find that you have to pull off the post-it notes and rearrange them, but that's perfectly fine.

*Reread the section in Part Two on Judging Your Progress.*

*Don't be too quick to push from one stage of concentration to the next.*

All too often, as soon as you attain a level of concentration, the mind asks a question of hunger: "What's next?" The best answer is, *"This* is what's next." Learn how to master what you've got. Meditation is not an exercise in jumping through jhana hoops. If you push impatiently from one level of concentration to the next, or if you try to analyze a new state of concentration too quickly after you've attained it, you never give it the chance to show its full potential. And you don't give yourself the chance to familiarize yourself with it. To get the most out of it, you need to keep working at it as a skill. Try to reach it quickly each time you start meditating. Try tapping into it in all situations. This enables you to see it from a variety of perspectives and to test it over time— to see if it really is as totally blissful, empty, and relaxed as it may have seemed at first sight.

If moving to a new level of concentration makes you feel unsteady, return to the level you just left and try to make it more firm before trying the new level again at a later time.

*If you're not sure about what to do at any stage in the concentration, simply stay with your sense of the "observer."*

Don't be too quick to jump to any conclusions about whether what you're doing is right or wrong, or whether what you're experiencing is true or false. Just watch, watch, watch. At the very least, you won't be taken in by false assumptions. And you may gain some important insights into how the mind can fool itself through its desire to label and interpret things.

*More important than labeling your concentration is learning what to do with it.*

Whether your concentration falls into the stages on the map or has a few different stages of its own, the proper way to treat any stage of concentration is the same in all cases. First, learn to maintain it as long as you can, in as many postures and activities as you can. Try to re-enter it as quickly as you can. This allows you to familiarize yourself with it. When you're really familiar with it, pull out of it slightly so that you can observe how the mind is relating to its object—but not so far out that you fully leave that stage of concentration. Some people experience this as "lifting" the mind slightly above its object. For others it feels like having your hand snugly in a glove and then pulling it out slightly so that it's not fully snug but still remains in the glove.

Either way, you're now in a position to observe the movements of the mind around the object of its concentration. Ask yourself a question of discernment: "Is there still any sense of disturbance or stress *in* the concentration itself?" The stress might be related to the fact that the mind is still evaluating its object when it no longer needs to, that it's holding onto rapture when the rapture is no longer calming, or that it's focused on a perception that's not as restful as it could be. If you can't immediately see any stress, try to notice any variations in the level of stress or disturbance you feel. This may take a while, but when you see a variation in the level of stress, try to see what activity of the mind accompanies the rises and falls of the stress. Once you identify the activity that accompanies the rises, drop it.

If you can't yet see any variation in the stress, or if your analysis starts getting blurry, it's a sign that your concentration isn't yet strong enough to engage in this kind of analysis. Drop the analysis and plant yourself firmly back in the object of your concentration. Don't be impatient. Stay with the object until you feel refreshed and solid enough to try the analysis again.

If, however, the analysis is getting clear results, keep it up. This will strengthen your concentration at the same time as it strengthens your discernment. You're learning how to evaluate your state of mind for yourself, while you're engaged in it, without having to consult any outside authority. You're gaining practice in observing how the mind creates unnecessary stress for itself, and in training it not to continue creating that stress. That's what the meditation is all about.

At the same time, you're mastering a line of questioning that—as your concentration and discernment grow deeper and subtler—gives rise to the insight leading to release.

## INSIGHT

As I noted in the Introduction, the basic strategy of the practice is to observe your actions—along with their motivations and results—and then to question them: Do they lead to suffering? If so, are they necessary? If not, how can you act in other ways that don't lead to suffering? If they don't lead to suffering, how can you master them as skills? This strategy applies not only to your words and deeds, but also to the acts of the mind: its thoughts and emotions.

And as I noted in the last section, when you develop jhana, you use this strategy of observing and questioning to abandon any distracting thoughts and to develop the factors of jhana in their place. It's through this process that the practice of jhana develops your discernment and insight. When your jhana becomes more stable, you can develop that insight further by looking for a course of action that causes even less stress than jhana. Here again, the important point is to view the factors of jhana as activities and to ask the right questions about them.

*Fabrication.* The activities here are the three types of fabrications by which the mind shapes experience: bodily, verbal, and mental. If you compare the descriptions of jhana and breath meditation with the descriptions of fabrication in the Introduction, you'll notice that jhana makes use of all three. The breath is bodily fabrication; the directed thought and evaluation of the first jhana are verbal fabrications; the perceptions that keep the mind in the various jhanas and formless attainments are mental fabrications, as are the feelings of pleasure and equanimity that come from staying in those states of concentration.

This is why jhana is so useful in giving rise to the insight that totally ends the unnecessary stress that the mind creates through its own fabrications. Jhana gives you a still vantage point for watching those fabrications in action.

You can do this in any of three ways:

- while you're in a particular stage of jhana;
- when you move from one stage to another; or
- when you come out of concentration and observe what fabrications the mind takes up as it engages with the world outside.

In any of these situations, you can observe that (1) fabrications are actually actions, arising and passing away; (2) they're creating stress; (3) what they're doing is unnecessary; and (4) the pleasure they give isn't worth the stress they entail. Only when you see all four of these aspects can insight lead to release from unnecessary suffering and stress. And that's when you see that the only stress weighing down the mind was the unnecessary sort. Once that stress is gone, nothing at all can weigh the mind down. It's free.

To watch any of the jhanas as forms of mental action requires *not* seeing them as metaphysical principles—say, as a Ground of Being, a True Self, Cosmic Oneness, Primordial Emptiness, Encounter with God, or any other grand-sounding abstraction. The metaphysical trap is an easy one to fall into, especially if you've primed yourself to think in those terms. If, for instance, you've been thinking in metaphysical terms and then attain the oneness of the second jhana, it's easy to assume that you've touched Cosmic Oneness or Interconnection. If you attain the sense of infinite knowing of the dimension of the infinitude of consciousness, it's easy to assume that you've gained access to a level of awareness underlying all reality. You might interpret these experiences as contact with some sort of ground from which all things come and to which they all return. Or you might decide that the strengthened sense of "observer" in that state of mind is your True Self. If you fall for any of these interpretations, though, you lose sight of the way in which your actions fashioned the experience to begin with. That way you miss the subtle levels of stress still present in those experiences. The exalted interpretations you assign to them blind you to the fabrications they still contain.

To get around this pitfall, you simply stick with the line of questioning introduced at the end of the last section: Look for any rise or fall in the level of stress within that experience. Then look for the activity of the mind that accompanies that rise and fall. When you see the activity in action, drop it.

This is called contemplating inconstancy and the stress in inconstancy. When you see the stress, ask yourself if anything inconstant and stressful is worth claiming as you or yours. When you realize that the answer is No, this is called contemplating not-self. You're not taking a stance on whether or not there is a self. You're simply asking whether you want to identify with the parts of the committee creating the stress.

**Developing disenchantment.** The purpose of these contemplations is to induce a sense of disenchantment and dispassion for the actions of fabrication. Because passion is what drives all three kinds of fabrication, dispassion ends any desire to keep engaging in them. When you don't engage in them, they stop. The result is a total letting go.

The sense of disenchantment—which in most cases reaches maturity only after you've approached these contemplations from many angles—is the crucial turning point in this process. The Pali term for disenchantment, *nibbida*, corresponds to the feeling you have when you've eaten enough of a particular food and don't want any more of it. This is not aversion. It's simply a sense that what you used to enjoy eating no longer holds any interest for you. You've had enough.

You need to develop this sense of disenchantment toward the mind's fabrications because they all follow the same pattern we've mentioned many times: They're a form of eating. The food here may be either physical or mental, but the dynamic of feeding in every case is the same. You're trying to fill a lack, to allay a hunger. Only when you can counteract the hunger with a sense of enough can you reach disenchantment. Only with disenchantment can you stop feeding and find the dimension where there's no need to feed.

**Insight into becoming.** Think back on the image of the mind's committee. Each committee member corresponds to a different desire, a different sense of who you are based around that desire, and a different sense of the world in which you can search for what will fulfill that desire. Your sense of who you are here is composed of two things: the self that will experience the happiness of fulfilling that desire, and the self that has the powers to bring that desire to fulfillment. The first self is the self as *consumer;* the second, the self as *producer.* The self as consumer is what needs to be fed; the self as producer is what finds and fixes the food; and the world of experience connected to the desire is the area of experience where you look for food.

As I noted in the Introduction, each individual sense of self in a particular world of experience is described by the term *becoming.* Becoming is a type of being—the sense of what you are and what exists around you—based on doing. It's not static being. It's being in action. And as you've been meditating, you've had plenty of opportunity to see how the primary action underlying this being is a kind of feeding. Each sense of who you are has to be nourished, to take something from the world, in order to survive.

You notice this first with the distracting thoughts that get in the way of your concentration: The mind goes out to nibble on thoughts of lust, to gobble down thoughts of anger, to sip pleasant memories from the past, to chew on past regrets, or to wolf down worries about the future.

The basic strategy of concentration is first to see that you don't have to identify with these different senses of who you are. That's why we use the image of the committee: to help you realize that you won't be starved of pleasure if you drop a few of these becomings. You've got better ones with which to feed. But then to keep yourself from sneaking out to chew on your old junk food, you have to nourish the more skillful members of the committee, the ones who are learning to work together to develop and maintain your concentration. This is one of the roles of the rapture, pleasure, and refined equanimity in concentration: to nourish the skillful members of your committee. When you practice concentration, you're feeding them good, nourishing food.

As you get less and less inclined to feed in your old ways—as your taste in inner food grows more refined—you gradually come to a point where you can see that even the concentration is a kind of becoming. In other words, in jhana you identify with the skillful members of the committee who can provide the food of concentration (the self as producer), as well as with the meditator feeding off the pleasure and rapture provided by the meditation (the self as consumer). The object of meditation—either the form of the body or the dimensions of formlessness—is the world from which you feed.

As long as you hold to these identities and these worlds as having solid unity, it's hard to go beyond them. It's hard to let go of them. This is why the Buddha's strategy is to sidestep this sense of solid unity by regarding the building blocks of identity as actions, for actions are easier to let go of than a solid sense of who you are.

**The five aggregates.** Because these actions are primarily related to feeding, the Buddha's approach in developing insight is to take the types of fabrication involved in creating every becoming and gather them under a list of five activities that are basic to feeding on every level.

These activities are called *khandhas*. This is a Pali word that means "heap" or "mass." The standard English translation, though, is "aggregate." This translation apparently comes from a distinction popular in eighteenth and nineteenth century Europe, between conglomerates of things that work together in an organic unity—called "systems"—and conglomerates that are just random collections of things, called "aggregates." The purpose of translating *khandha* as "aggregate" was to convey the useful point that even though we tend to regard our sense of identity as having organic unity, it's actually just a random collection of activities.

The five activities that surround eating on the most basic level are these:

• A sense of *form*: both the form of the body that needs to be nourished (and that will be used to look for food), as well as the physical objects that will be used as food. When feeding takes place in the imagination, "form" applies to whatever form you assume for yourself in the imagination, and to whatever imaginary forms you take pleasure from.

• *Feeling*: the painful feeling of hunger or lack that drives you to look for food; the pleasant feeling of satisfaction that comes when you've found something to eat; and the added pleasure when you actually eat it.

• *Perception*: the ability to identify the type of hunger you feel, and to identify which of the things in your world of experience will satisfy that hunger. Perception also plays a central role in identifying what is and isn't food. This is the way we first learn to exercise our perceptions as children. Our first reaction on encountering something is to put it into our mouth to see if it's edible. If it is, we label it with the perception of "food." If it's not, we label it as "not food."

• *Fabrication* in this context refers primarily to verbal fabrications. These relate to feeding in the way we have to think about and evaluate strategies for finding food, for taking possession of it when we find it, and for fixing it if it's not edible in its raw state. For example, if you want to enjoy a banana, you have to figure out how to remove the peel. If your first attempt doesn't work, you have to evaluate why it didn't and to figure out new strategies until you find one that works.

• *Consciousness:* the act of being aware of all these activities.

These five activities are so basic to the way we engage with the world in order to feed that they form the raw material from which we create our various senses of self.

Now, in the practice of developing jhana based on the breath, they're also the raw material from which we've learned to create states of concentration. "Form" corresponds to the breath. "Feeling" corresponds to the feelings of pleasure and equanimity derived from focusing on the breath. "Perception" corresponds to the ways we label the breath, the formless dimensions, and the pleasures we derive from staying focused on these themes. "Fabrication" corresponds to the thoughts and evaluations that compose the first jhana, and also the thoughts and evaluations by which we ask questions about all the various stages in our concentration. "Consciousness" is the act of being aware of all these activities.

This is why concentration is such a good laboratory for examining the mind's habits for creating suffering. It contains all the elements that go into the identities we build around the act of feeding. And it contains them in a controlled context—a clear and stable state of becoming—where you can watch those elements in action and see them clearly for what they are.

When the mind is in a solid enough position to look at even the refined pleasures of concentration in terms of these activities, there's no need to focus on all five of them. Simply focus on any one that seems easiest for you to observe in action. If you're not sure of where to start, try starting with perception, because perception is most central to your ability to stay focused in concentration, and it's the aggregate you're going to need to work hardest to change. As long as the perception, "worth the effort," stays fixed on the act of feeding on jhana, disenchantment will not be total. Only when the perception, "not worth the effort," gets your full approval will disenchantment have a chance.

Still, this is a matter of personal temperament. If another aggregate seems easier to focus on, by all means start there, for once the perception of "not worth the effort" gets firmly established with regard to that aggregate, it will spread to encompass all the other aggregates because all five of them are so intimately connected.

When examining the activities that create states of concentration, you have to remember to ask the right questions about them. If you approach the concentration in hopes that it will answer such questions as "Who am I?" or "What is the underlying reality of the world?", you simply continue the processes of becoming. If you come across an especially impressive state of stillness or peace, your committee members who want to feed on metaphysical absolutes will take that as their food—and will be mighty proud of it. This blinds you to the fact that they're still just feeding, and that your questions are simply refined versions of the questions of hunger.

However, if you remember to see the stillness and peace of concentration as coming from the activities of the aggregates, you'll realize that no matter how well you feed on them, you'll never be free of reoccurring hunger. You'll never be free of having to keep working for your food. After all, these activities are not constant. When they fall away, they produce a split second of concern: "What's next?" And in that split second, your committee members are desperate, for the question is a question of hunger. They want an answer *right now*. So these activities can never provide a stable, reliable, or lasting food. Even when they fabricate a peace that feels cosmic, they still involve stress.

When you pursue these contemplations until they reach a point of disenchantment, the mind inclines toward something outside of space and time, something that wouldn't be subject to the drawbacks of these activities. At this point, it wants nothing to do with any of the committee members of the mind, even the ones observing and directing its concentration, or the underlying ones that keep asking and demanding an answer to the questions of hunger: "What's next? Where next? What to do next?" The mind sees that even the choice of staying in place or moving forward to another state of concentration—even though it's a choice between two relatively skillful alternatives—is a choice between nothing but two stressful alternatives, for both are fabrications. At this point it's poised for something that doesn't involve either alternative, something that involves no fabrication. When it sees the opening in that poise, it lets go and experiences the deathless. That's the first stage in experiencing release.

In this way, the mind dis-identifies with all becomings without even thinking about "self" or "worlds." It looks simply at actions as actions. It sees them as stressful, unnecessary, and not worth the effort. That's what enables it to let go.

### RELEASE

There are many dangers in trying to describe release, for people can then easily try to clone the description without actually going through the steps leading to genuine release—another case of squeezing and painting the mango to make it ripe.

However, it *is* useful to describe some of the lessons learned from the first taste of release.

One is that the Buddha was right: There really is a deathless dimension, outside of space and time. And it really is free of suffering and stress.

On returning from that dimension into the dimensions of space and time, you realize that your experience of space and time didn't begin just with this birth. It's been going on much longer. You may not be able to remember the particulars of previous lifetimes, but you do know that they've been happening for a long, long time.

Because you reached that dimension by abandoning the activities of fabrication, you know that it was through the activities of fabrication that you have been engaged in space and time all along. In other words, you're not just a passive observer of space and time. Your actions play a crucial role in shaping your experience of space and time. Your actions are thus of foremost importance. Because you see that unskillful actions simply make it more difficult to access the deathless, you never want to break the five precepts ever again.

Because none of the aggregates were involved in the experience of the deathless, and yet there was still an awareness of that dimension, you see that the act of identifying with the aggregates is a choice that places limitations on you. You'll never again agree with the view that they constitute what you are.

Because you realize that the deathless dimension was always available, but that you missed it because of your own stupidity, the first taste of release is humbling. It's not a source of pride.

But above all, you realize that the activities of engaging in space and time are inherently stressful. The only true happiness lies in gaining total release. There is no activity more worthwhile than that.

It's important not to mistake a mundane breakthrough for genuine release, for that can make you heedless and complacent in your practice. One of the touchstones for testing the truth of your release is whether it feels grounding or disorienting. If it's disorienting, it's not the real thing, for the deathless is the safest, most secure dimension there is.

Another touchstone for testing the truth of your release is whether you understood what you did to get there, for that's what provides insight into the role of fabrication and mental action in shaping all experience. If your mind senses a great unburdening but without understanding how it happened, it's not release. It's just a mundane breakthrough. So don't be heedless.

However, even people who have attained their first taste of genuine release can grow heedless, as the safety of their attainment can lower their sense of urgency in the practice. They can start getting complacent. So whether your sense that you've tasted release is genuine or not, the advice is always the same: Don't be heedless. There's more work to do.

*Additional readings:*

On jhana: See the section, "Jhana," in Ajaan Lee Dhammadharo, *Keeping the Breath in Mind,* "Method 2." There are also excellent discussions of jhana in Ajaan Lee's book, *The Path to Peace & Freedom for the Mind,* under the heading, "Right Concentration" and under the headings of "Virtue," "Concentration," and "Discernment" at the end of the book.

See also the article, "Jhana Not by the Numbers," and the talk, "Oneness" in *Meditations4.*

For a thorough discussion of the Buddha's sixteen-step instructions for using the breath as a focal point for developing tranquility and insight, see *Right Mindfulness.*

For a more advanced discussion of the role of becoming, both in the practice of jhana and in the development of insight, see *The Paradox of Becoming.*

On insight: "One Tool Among Many"; "The Integrity of Emptiness"; "All About Change"

On the aggregates: "Five Piles of Bricks"; "De-perception"

On the relationship between feeding and stress: "The Weight of Mountains." For a more advanced discussion of this topic, see Chapter Two in *The Shape of Suffering.*

For further discussions on how to ask the questions of discernment: Somewhat more technical than "Questions of Skill," mentioned at the end of the Introduction, is "The Arrows of Thinking." *Skill in Questions* offers a full treatment of this topic, with many examples from the Pali Canon. If the size of the book puts you off, you can read just the discussions in each chapter and leave the readings for another time.

For an anthology of passages from the Pali Canon covering the basic qualities that the Buddha said were most important for the practice, see *The Wings to Awakening*. Some people find the Introduction to this book a little steep, but you can start with Part Three, which is less intimidating, and then return to the earlier parts of the book when you want a more extensive overview.

*Into the Stream* contains passages from the Pali Canon on the first stage of awakening.

On release as the essence of the practice: "The Essence of the Dhamma"

On the meaning of the word *nirvana*: "The Image of Nirvana"; "A Verb for Nirvana." *The Mind like Fire Unbound* offers a full treatment of this topic, along with a discussion of the topic of clinging.

For some inspiring accounts of higher stages of the practice, see Ajaan MahaBoowa Ñanasampanno – *Straight from the Heart,* in particular the talks, "At the End of One's Rope," "The Radiant Mind is Unawareness," and "An Heir to the Dhamma." Also inspiring: "From Ignorance to Emptiness" and "To Be an Inner Millionaire," both in another book of Ajaan MahaBoowa's talks, *Things as They Are.*

Inspiring in a more calming way are these talks in Ajaan Lee Dhammadharo, *Inner Strength:* "Beyond Right & Wrong"; and "Point Zero."

*Relevant talks:*

2009/1/30: THE FOUR JHANAS
2011/8/21: THE POISON BLOWFISH
2011/9/4: PROACTIVE WITH PAIN
2011/3/10: THE SWINGING BALANCE
2009/2/14: A RECIPE FOR JHANA

*Talks on the Buddha's sixteen-step instructions in breath meditation:*

PART FIVE

# Finding a Teacher

Every earnest meditator needs a teacher. Because meditation is training in new ways to act, you learn best when you can watch an experienced meditator in action and at the same time can let an experienced meditator watch *you* in action. That way you tap into the accumulated wisdom of the lineage of teachers stretching back to the Buddha, and don't have to work through every problem completely on your own. You don't have to keep reinventing the Dhamma wheel from scratch.

At the same time, a teacher is often needed to help you see areas of your practice that you may not recognize as problems. This is because, when you're deluded, you don't *know* you're deluded. So one of the basic principles of the practice is to open your behavior not only to your own scrutiny but also to the scrutiny of a teacher whose knowledge and goodwill you trust. That way you learn how to be open with others—and yourself— about your mistakes, in an environment where you're most likely to be willing to learn.

This is especially important when you're learning a skill— which is what meditation is. You can learn from books and talks, but when the time comes to practice you'll encounter the main issue that no book or talk can cover: knowing how to judge which lesson to apply to which situation. If you're not getting results, is it because you're not putting in enough effort? Or are you making the wrong sort of effort? In the words of the Pali Canon, are you squeezing a cow's horn in the effort to get milk when you should be squeezing the udder? Only someone who has faced the same problem, and who knows what you've been doing, is in a position to help you answer questions like these.

Also, if you've suffered emotional trauma or are dealing with an addiction, you need guidance specifically tailored to your strengths and weaknesses—something no book can provide. Even if you don't suffer from these issues, a teaching tailored to your needs can save you a lot of wasted time and effort, and can help prevent you from going down some wrong, dead-end roads. This is why the Buddha didn't write meditation guides like this, and instead set up the monastic training as a form of apprenticeship. Meditation skills are best passed down person-to-person.

For these reasons, if you really want to become skillful in your thoughts, words, and deeds, you need to find a trustworthy teacher to point out your blind spots. And because those spots are blindest around your unskillful habits, the primary duty of the teacher is to point out your faults—for only when you see your faults can you correct them; only when you correct them are you benefiting from your teacher's compassion in pointing them out.

This means that the first prerequisite in benefiting from a teacher is being willing to take criticism, both gentle and harsh. This is why genuine teachers don't teach for money. If the teacher must be paid, the person paying is the one determining what's taught, and people rarely pay for the criticism they need to hear.

But even if the teacher is teaching for free, you run into an uncomfortable truth: *You can't open your heart to just anyone.* Not everyone who is certified as a teacher is really qualified to be a teacher. When you listen to a teacher, you're adding that teacher's voice to the committee of your mind, passing judgments on your actions, so you want to make sure that that voice will be a positive addition. As the Buddha pointed out, *if you can't find a trustworthy teacher, you're better off practicing on your own.* An unqualified teacher can do more harm than good. You have to take care in choosing a teacher whose judgments will influence the way you shape your mind.

To take care means not falling into the easy trap of being judgmental or non-judgmental—judgmental in trusting your knee-jerk likes or dislikes, non-judgmental in trusting that every meditation teacher would be equally beneficial as a guide. Instead, be *judicious* in choosing the person whose judgments you're going to take on as your own.

This, of course, sounds like a Catch-22: You need a good teacher to help develop your powers of judgment, but well-developed powers of judgment to recognize who a good teacher might be. And even though there's no foolproof way out of the catch—after all, you can master a foolproof way and still be a fool—there *is* a way if you're willing to learn from experience.

The first step in learning to be judicious is to remember what it means to judge in a helpful way. Think, not of a Supreme Court Justice sitting on her bench, passing a final verdict of guilt or innocence, but of a piano teacher listening to you play. She's not passing a final verdict on your potential as a pianist. Instead, she's judging a work in progress: listening to your intention for the performance, listening to your execution of that intention, and then deciding whether it works. If it doesn't, she has to figure out if the problem is with the intention or the execution, make helpful suggestions, and then let you try again. She keeps this up until she's satisfied with your performance. The important principle is that she never direct her judgments at you as a person. Instead she has to stay focused on your actions, to keep looking for better ways to raise them to higher and higher standards.

At the same time, you're learning from her how to judge your own playing: thinking more carefully about your intention, listening more carefully to your execution, developing higher standards for what works, and learning to think outside of the box for ways to improve. Most important of all, you're learning to focus your judgment on your performance—your actions—and not on yourself. This way, when there's less *you* invested in your habits, you're more willing to recognize unskillful habits and to drop them in favor of more skillful ones. Of course, when you and your teacher are judging your improvement on a particular piece, it's part of a longer process of judging how well the relationship is working. She has to judge, over time, if you're benefiting from her guidance, and so do you. But again, neither of you is judging the worth of the other person.

In the same way, when you're evaluating a potential meditation teacher, look for someone who will evaluate your actions as a work in progress. And apply the same standard to him or her. Even teachers who can read minds need to get to know you over time to sense what might and might not work in your particular case. The best teachers are those who say, "Try this. If it doesn't work out, come back and let me know what happened, so we can figure out what might work for you." Beware of teachers who tell you not to think about what you're doing, or who try to force you into a one-size-fits-all technique. The relationship should be one of trying things out together.

So when judging a teacher, you're not trying to take on the superhuman role of evaluating another person's essential worth. After all, the only way we know anything about other people is through their actions, so that's as far as our judgments can fairly extend.

At the same time, though, because you're judging whether you want to internalize another person's standards, it's not unfair to pass judgment on what that person is doing. It's for your own protection. This is why you should look for two qualities in a teacher: *wisdom and integrity*. To gauge these qualities, though, takes time and sensitivity. You have to be willing to spend time with the person and try to be really observant of how that person acts, because you can't judge people just by first impressions. Integrity is easy to talk about, and the appearance of wisdom is easy to fake—especially if the teacher has psychic powers. It's important to remember that powers of that sort simply come from a concentrated mind. They're no guarantee of wisdom and integrity. And if they're exercised without wisdom and integrity, you're better off staying away.

So your search has to ignore flashy qualities and focus on qualities that are more plain and down-to-earth. To save time and needless pain in the search, there are *four early warning signs* indicating that potential teachers don't have the wisdom or integrity to merit your trust.

The warning signs for untrustworthy wisdom are two. The first is when people *show no gratitude* for the help they've received—and this applies especially to help from their parents and teachers. If they deprecate their teachers, you have to wonder if they have anything of value to pass on to you. People with no gratitude don't appreciate goodness, don't value the effort that goes into being helpful, and so will probably not put out that effort themselves.

The second warning sign is that they *don't hold to the principle of karma.* They either deny that we have freedom of choice, or else teach that one person can clear away another person's bad karma from the past. People of this sort are unlikely to put forth the effort to be genuinely skillful, and so are untrustworthy guides.

Lack of integrity also has two warning signs. The first is when people *feel no shame in telling a deliberate lie.* The second is when they *don't conduct arguments in a fair and aboveboard manner:* misrepresenting their opponents, pouncing on the other side's minor lapses, not acknowledging the valid points the other side has made. People of this sort aren't even worth talking to, much less taking on as teachers.

As for people who don't display these early warning signs, there are some questions you can ask yourself about their behavior to gauge the level of wisdom and integrity in their actions over time.

One question is whether a teacher's actions betray any of the greed, anger, or delusion that would inspire him to claim knowledge of something he didn't know, or to tell another person to do something that was not in that person's best interests. To test for a teacher's wisdom, notice how he or she responds to questions about what's skillful and what's not, and how well he or she handles adversity. To test for integrity, look for virtue in day-to-day activities, and purity in the teacher's dealings with others. Does this person make excuses for breaking the precepts, bringing the precepts down to his level of behavior rather than lifting his behavior to theirs? Does he take unfair advantage of other people? If so, you'd better find another teacher.

This, however, is where another uncomfortable truth comes in: *You can't be a fair judge of another person's integrity until you've developed some of your own.* This is probably the most uncomfortable truth of all, for it requires that you accept responsibility for your judgments. If you want to test other people's potential for good guidance, you have to pass a few tests yourself. Again, it's like listening to a pianist. The better you are as a pianist, the better your ability to judge the other person's playing.

Fortunately, there are guidelines for developing integrity, and they don't require that you start out innately good. All they require is a measure of truthfulness and maturity: the realization that your actions make all the difference in your life, so you have to take care in how you act, looking carefully at your motivation for acting and at the actual results that come when you act. Before you act in thought, word, or deed, look at the results you expect from your action. If it's going to harm you or anyone else, don't do it. If you don't foresee any harm, go ahead and act. While you're acting, check to see if you're causing any unforeseen harm. If you are, stop. If not, continue until you're done. After you're done, look at the long-term results of your action. If it caused any harm, talk it over with someone else on the path, develop a healthy sense of shame around the mistake, and resolve not to repeat it. If it caused no harm, take joy in the fact and keep on training.

As you train yourself in this way, you get more sensitive to what is and isn't skillful, because you're more sensitive to the connections between actions and their results. This helps you become a better judge of a potential teacher in two ways, both in judging the teacher's actions and in evaluating the advice the teacher gives you.

For the only way really to evaluate that advice is to see what results it gives when put into action: your own actions. If acting in that way fosters within you such admirable qualities as being dispassionate, modest, content, energetic, and unburdensome, the advice to act that way is the genuine thing. The person who gives you that advice has passed at least that test for being a genuine friend. And you're learning still more about how to judge for yourself.

Some people might object that it's selfish and inhumane to keep testing people to see if they fit the bill, but remember: In testing a teacher you're also testing yourself. As you assimilate the qualities of an admirable teacher, you become the sort of person who can offer admirable help to others. Again, it's like practicing under a good piano teacher. As you improve as a pianist, you're not the only one who can enjoy your playing. The better you get, the more joy you bring to others. The better you understand the process of playing, the more effectively you can teach anyone who sincerely wants to learn from you. This is how teaching lineages of high caliber get established for the benefit of the world.

So when you find an admirable meditation teacher, you're tapping into a long lineage of admirable teachers, stretching back to the Buddha, and helping it to extend into the future. Joining this lineage may require accepting some uncomfortable truths, such as the need to learn from criticism and to take responsibility for your actions. But if you're up for the challenge, you learn to take this

human power of judgment—which, when untrained, can so easily
cause harm—and train it for the greater good.

*Additional readings:*

On the need for advice in the practice: "Lost in Quotation"
On the most important external factor in reaching awaken-
ing: "Admirable Friendship" in *Meditations*
On wise *vs.* unwise ways of using your powers of judgment,
see "Judicious *vs.* Judgmental" in *Meditations*
On the teacher-student relationship: "Think like a Thief"
Passages from the Pali Canon discussing what to look for in a
teacher are included in the study guide, *Into the Stream.*
On the values of the practice: "The Customs of the Noble
Ones"
On non-Buddhist values that have shaped the way Dhamma is
often taught in the West: *Buddhist Romanticism*

*Relevant talks:*

2009/7/30: ADMIRABLE FRIENDSHIP
2011/5/14: TO PURIFY THE HEART
2011/4/5: REMEMBERING AJAAN SUWAT
2011/1/25: MULTI-DIMENSIONAL DHAMMA
2007/7/21: FACTORS FOR STREAM ENTRY
2008/10/21: THE BRIGHTNESS OF THE WORLD
2007/3/20: A REFUGE FROM MODERN VALUES

APPENDIX

# Supplementary Meditations

As I noted in Part One, there are times when you need to get the mind in the right mood before it will be willing to settle down with the breath. Here are a few contemplations that can help create that mood.

The explanations here are simply suggestions for how to get started with these contemplations, for these exercises are most effective when you use your ingenuity to tailor them to deal with the particulars of your own moods. You can make any variations you want, as long as they help move your thinking in the right direction: toward a desire to settle down with the breath. When that desire arises, you can drop the contemplation and focus right on your breathing.

In the beginning, you may find that you need to engage for a fairly long time in these contemplations before they have an effect. Eventually, though, you should gain a sense of what works for you. Use that knowledge to make your contemplation more efficient. In other words, go right for the jugular of the mind state that's getting in the way of your settling down. That way you'll have more time to work and play with the breath.

**When you're feeling discouraged,** try reflecting on your own *generosity*. Think of times in the past when you gave someone a gift, not because you had to or because it was expected of you, but because you simply wanted to. You had something that you would have liked to use yourself, but then you decided you'd rather share it. Gifts of this sort are good to remember because they remind you that you do have at least *some* goodness to yourself. They also remind you that you're not always a slave to your appetites. You have some freedom in how you act, and some experience in how good it feels to exercise that freedom in a skillful way. The word "gift" here doesn't mean only a material gift. It can also mean a gift of your time, your energy, your knowledge, or your forgiveness.

To get the most out of this contemplation, make a habit of looking for opportunities in your daily life to be generous in any of these ways. That way you always have fresh material for your contemplation. Without fresh material, the contemplation can quickly grow stale.

In a similar way, you can reflect on your own *virtue*. Think of times when you could have gotten away with harming someone else, but you didn't do it. On principle. You saw that it was beneath you or would have led to regret down the line. If you've taken the precepts, reflect on the times when you were tempted to break any of them, but you managed not to. Think of how glad you are, in retrospect, that you didn't. This sort of reflection not only helps the mind settle down in concentration, but also helps you resist any temptations to break a precept the next time they come around.

**When you're feeling lustful,** contemplate what's inside your body, and remember that the same things are in the person for whose body you're feeling lust. Remember that lust can grow only when you block out huge areas of reality—such as all the contents of the body—so broaden the range of your inner gaze.

To get some beginning practice with this contemplation, try visualizing the bones in your body. Start with the bones of the fingers. As you visualize them, ask where you feel your fingers are right now. If there's any tension in the fingers, remember that there's no tension in the bones, so relax the tension. Then move up to the bones in the palm of your hand, and repeat the same exercise: Notice the tension around the bones and relax it. Keep moving up the arms, repeating the same exercise, until you reach the shoulders. When you've contemplated the shoulder joints, move your inner gaze down to your feet. As you visualize the bones in your feet, relax any tension you feel in the feet. Then move up the legs, through the pelvis, up the spine, through the neck, and finally to the skull.

As a variation on this exercise, once you've finished relaxing a part of the body around a particular bone, visualize it being lopped off as you move to the next part. Keep this up until every part of the body feels lopped away, and you're sitting with a sense of spacious, light awareness.

You can apply the same exercise to any other organ of the body that you find especially incongruous with your lust. If, for instance, you find yourself attracted to skin, imagine your skin removed from your body and placed in a pile on the floor.

To aid in your visualization, you can memorize the traditional list of body parts used in this sort of contemplation:

head hairs, body hairs, nails, teeth, skin;
muscle, tendons, bones, bone marrow;
kidneys, heart, liver, membranes, spleen, lungs;
large intestines, small intestines, contents of the stomach,
    feces;
bile, phlegm, lymph, blood, sweat, fat, tears;
oil, saliva, mucus, fluid in the joints, urine.

If you want, you can add other parts—such as the eyes or the brain—that for some reason didn't make it into the traditional list. Once you've memorized the list, visualize the parts one by one, asking yourself—with each part—where that part is in your felt sense of the body. To help with your visualization, you can look at an anatomical chart, but remember that none of the parts in your body are cleanly separate and defined as they would be in such a chart. They're mixed with all the fluids in the body. If visualizing a particular part has a particularly strong effect in counteracting lust, you can focus your primary attention on that part and, for the time being, put the rest of the list aside. (For further ideas on dealing with lust, look at the discussion of Disruptive Emotions in Part Two.) Ideally, this contemplation should give rise to an inner sense of lightness as you lose interest in the lust. If, however, you find it giving rise to fear or unsettling emotions, drop it and return to the breath.

**When you're feeling angry,** look at the instructions for dealing with anger in Part Two. You can also try the instructions for developing the brahmaviharas, in Part One.

**When you're feeling lazy,** contemplate the fact that death could come at any time. Ask yourself: Are you ready to go in the next minute or two? What would you need to do to put your mind in a state where it wouldn't be afraid to die? How would you feel if you died tonight after wasting the opportunity to meditate and develop good strong qualities in the mind? Keep asking yourself questions along these lines until you feel a desire to meditate. Then go straight to the breath.

This contemplation, like the contemplation of the body, is meant to strengthen the mind in skillful resolves. If, however, you find that it gives rise to fear or unsettling emotions, drop it and go straight to the breath.

Another antidote to laziness is to think of times in the past when you wished you could find a moment of peace and quiet. Think of how desperate you felt at those times. Now you've got the opportunity to find that peace and quiet. Do you want to throw it away?

*Additional readings:*

For some helpful texts on these contemplations, see the study guide, *The Ten Recollections,* also available under the title, *A Meditator's Tools.* See also: "Under Your Skin."

# ACKNOWLEDGEMENTS

For years, a handful of people—in particular, Mary Talbot, Jane Yudelman, Bok Lim Kim, and Larry Rosenberg—have been asking me, "When are you going to do a guide on breath meditation?" I kept telling them that Ajaan Lee's *Keeping the Breath in Mind* is already an excellent guide to the practice, but they kept insisting in return that there's a need for a book written specifically for a reader without a background in the Thai Wilderness Tradition. Their gentle but persistent pressure is what has brought this book into being. Now that the book is a reality, I want to thank them, for I've learned a lot in trying to gather my thoughts on the topic into a concise, accessible form.

The book has benefitted from their comments on it, as well as from comments by Ajahn Nyanadhammo, Michael Barber, Matthew Grad, Ruby Grad, Katharine Greider, Addie Onsanit, Nathanial Osgood, Dale Schulz, Joe Thitathan, Donna Todd, Josephine Wolf, Barbara Wright, and the monks here at the monastery. I would like to thank them for their help. Any errors in the book, of course, are my own.

*December, 2012*